Best
D0863324

Best Canadian Essays 2016

SERIES EDITOR
Christopher Doda

GUEST EDITOR
Joseph Kertes

TIGHTROPE BOOKS

Tightrope Books
#207-2 College Street,
Toronto Ontario, Canada M5G 1K3
tightropebooks.com
bookinfo@tightropebooks.com

SERIES EDITOR: Christopher Doda
GUEST EDITOR: Joseph Kertes
MANAGING EDITOR: Heather Wood
COVER AND INTERIOR DESIGN: David Jang

We thank the Canada Council for the Arts and the Ontario Arts Council for their support of our publishing program.

Printed and bound in Canada.

A cataloguing record for this publication is available from Library and Archives Canada.

CONTENTS

Preface

Essays get a bad rap. confronted with the word 'essay,' I suspect many in Canada have dim and regrettable memories of a beleaguered low-year high school teacher attempting to elucidate the dreaded five paragraph essay format (introduction, second best point, weakest point, strongest point, conclusion). Or perhaps many quail at even earlier memories of elementary school compositions along the lines of 'what I did on my summer vacation.' The noted American essayist Phillip Lopate has stated that he was once "turned off" the essay form because of how it was presented to him, that "it had been taught in freshman composition mainly as a way to hone argumentative skills and defend a position in an academic paper or debate" as opposed to an exploration of an experience or an idea (especially noticeable in the United States as essay teaching is geared almost exclusively to the 'Common App' essay on college applications). In other words, teaching around the essay has long been stale and programmatic. I can certainly vouch from my own distant school experience that the five paragraph format was taught as the only option, instead of as a foundation for more creative possibilities. Of course, antipathy to the essay is not new. In his introduction to the 1935 anthology *Essays in Modern Thought*, Thomas R. Cook implored the reader "not to be frightened by a word on a book cover" even if "one is apt to think instinctively, in connection with essay-reading, of a wordy treatise, formal and probably dry, headed by the austere signature of a Francis Bacon." If this guilt by (mental) association is as pervasive as I think it is, it's no wonder the word seems to give people hives.

To translate such ill-will and discontent into commercial sales is an even greater uphill task. Getting people to flash the plastic for a form of writing that invokes bad memories has long been a conundrum of the publishing industry. In "Bazaar," Croatian essayist Dubravka Ugresic relates a pitch meeting to a prominent editor about one of her collections:

"Essays, you say."

"Yes," I said as concisely as I could.

"And you say it just like that?"

"What do you mean?"

"I mean you say that so calmly, as though it were self-explanatory."

"I don't understand…"

"It's as though you were offering me a volume of poetry without a flicker of embarrassment!" the editor said angrily.

"What's wrong with a volume of poetry?"

"What planet do you live on! It doesn't sell, that's what! Hopeless. Just like essays!"

"OK," I said meekly.

To be ranked alongside poetry in terms of marketable appeal—and I am intimately familiar with the diminutive world of poetry, Canadian poetry in particular—is a body blow that all attempts at healing will resist. And yet, I have hope. Even back in 1935, Cook noticed that "all of us read essays as chosen fare in the newspapers and current magazines—only they are not headed by the dreaded term, Essay." I sometimes wonder if change in terminology would help.

While it may not be as commercially off-putting, unfortunately I have always found the term 'non-fiction' problematic at best and somewhat absurd at worst. It certainly privileges the novel and short story over the essay and the treatise as art forms. Moreover, built into the very word is the assumption that fiction is the dominant mode of prose and that non-fiction is an afterthought. As any linguist will say, trying to define something by what it is not is a fool's game. Besides, as this year's guest editor Joseph Kertes has eloquently demonstrated, the distinction between fiction and non-fiction is fairly blurry as both are dependent on narrative craft and techniques for their forcefulness. A non-fiction reader picks up a book for information certainly but also for the way it is imparted, its flow and style, something more akin to fiction. So we may be stuck with 'essay' for a while yet.

As I write this the 2016 Rio de Janeiro Olympics are winding down and it has me thinking of the idea of excellence. Canada placed tenth overall with 22 medals, a major feat in a summer games for a winter country. Elite performers of any stripe often have to produce brilliantly under tight conditions. One misstep or tactical error can mean the difference between first place and tenth. While writers don't have their status measured by hundredths of a second (or get medals and a place on a cereal box if they emerge victorious), they too must perform within strict parameters. The sixteen pieces in this current volume surely fit the bill. Whether they be personal remembrances or memoirs, topical essays, literary criticism or standard journalism, all have executed exceptionally well within the restrictions of the essay format. And like elite athletes, they sometimes need to push or modify the rules in order to succeed.

Whether the word graces this volume or not, it is in this idea of excellence that these essays have been deemed the 'best' of their year. (I imagine I am preaching to the converted though: if you have picked up the book and read this far, you are clearly not the sort of person to be intimidated by a word on a cover. Rest easy, Thomas R. Cook.) Whatever the reader's preferred term or not, in the upcoming pages they'll find works that override any concerns about whatever an essay is. The pieces here exhibit a range of complex emotions, are both informative and entertaining, intelligent and highly readable, with a depth that belies their concentrated form. If 'essay' gets a bad rap, so be it. If the Olympics teach us one thing every time around, it's that people love to root for an underdog.

Christopher Doda

Introduction

I CAME AT each of the essays and articles written in this country over the past year with three requirements: that the piece be an important addition to the work on the subject; that it be well-written—beautifully written is even better, a work of literature; and that it survive to be read years from now, if not decades (of course, the last one is the most difficult to predict).

An additional requirement for me is how good the story is. I know it is non-fiction we are considering, but if the author is unable to build the drama or humour or conflict or uncertainty or urgency into the piece, then the piece, for me, often falters. The art of non-fiction lies in the storytelling ability of its creator, just as it does in fiction. I want to feel compelled to read it, compelled to know. Tim O'Brien called this quality "forward tilt." Even if you don't know where you're going exactly, you know you want to get there. The piece has to have a kind of inevitability to it.

In fact, the difference between non-fiction and fiction is not that great, or at least not that discernable. Henry David Thoreau, who wrote one of the greatest non-fiction works ever, *Walden*, was not so much an outdoorsman as he was a writer (an indoorsman). He didn't sleep under the stars quite as often as he did at Emerson's place. He was a philosopher, a transcendentalist, an abolitionist.

He invented modern civil disobedience. Nature simply presented the best setting for his thoughts, the best backdrop.

Great non-fiction writers are more interested in telling the best story they can than they are in getting the story entirely right, with all of its boring bits included. Even if they try to be scrupulously truthful and correct, they are still going to leave out details they don't think are relevant or captivating. This selection process alone begins to move the non-fiction writer closer to the murky world of the writer of fiction. I submit that the best non-fiction writing depends on ability, not honesty. If non-fiction writers are to tell the truest story they can, they might have to bend the truth now and again to do so. They might have to enlarge the truth or deepen it to get at what they're really after. Simple facts and events often begin as mere anecdotes, and the writer has to find the larger meaning beneath these to tell the whole story. In other words, sometimes the simple facts of a story are too superficial, meaning the writer has to build a bigger, darker house to accommodate her/his sad tale.

Famously, Tim O'Brien's "On the Rainy River" tells the story of the day he got his draft notice to go to Vietnam. The "character" is called Tim O'Brien. He is spending his summer at home in Minnesota, working in a pig slaughterhouse when he learns he is to head off to war. He goes home, showers, takes the family car and heads northward toward Canada. When he gets to the Rainy River, a man named Elroy is closing down his fishing lodge—Tip Top Lodge, it is called. Tim asks if he can stay a few days, and Elroy lets him, as long as Tim helps him clean up and batten down the hatches for the fall. Elroy asks no questions. They get along well, play cards and board games; then, several days later, Elroy invites Tim to go fishing on the Rainy River. Elroy drops anchor twenty yards from the border. Tim describes how he stared longingly at Canada. He could almost touch it. He could see the latticework of the branches, the red berries in the bushes. But then Tim asks Elroy to take him back. He says, "I did the cowardly thing and went to Vietnam."

The only thing about this sad story is that it is untrue. O'Brien said, "You have to tell the truth in fiction, even if you have to lie." The day he got his induction notice to go to Vietnam, he was, in fact, golfing with his pals. But the weight of the realization of what awaited him was more fully and truly conveyed in the story of Elroy and the Rainy River. He had to find a setting big enough and dark enough to explore his true feelings on the subject. And he did so after returning from that horrible war.

It is in this story about "Tim O'Brien" that non-fiction and fiction writers meet. The only real difference is intent. Non-fiction writers set out to tell the truth, but sometimes they have to use their imaginations to get at it.

Two pieces in this collection get closest to what I'm talking about. One is Richard Kelly Kemick's "Playing God," in which the author talks about the magical Christmas village he creates on his mother's dining room table and thereby reconstructs the warmth and joys of his childhood. "I am filled so full with wanting," he says. "It is all I know." The second is Leona Theis' "Six Ways She Might Have Died before She Reached Nineteen." As the title suggests, the author ranges over events in her life that might have turned out differently—badly, actually. "Not everyone gets out alive," she tells us. It's another story about memory and how different life might have turned out if the author had taken a different route. "Life goes on," she writes, while memory stays the same, or is lit differently by the imagination.

Memory plays a big role in a number of the pieces. In Susan Olding's "White Matter," the ineffable relationship between author and reader, between artist and sensitive receiver of that art takes on new meaning: "the brain," she writes, "moves remarkably fast for an organ with the consistency of a slug." Olding remembers reading *Oliver Twist* at the age of twelve and knows now what the experience meant to her. The brain "learns, adapts, expands, creates. It can invent an enduring story that evokes a world for someone thousands of miles and hundreds of years away; it can read that story and grow, in the course of an afternoon, from a gormless larva of a girl to a creature endowed with wings." Michelle Kaesar's "A Dozen Cups of the Dead" is a consideration of a life, the author's father's in this case, and what he meant to her and her family. She finds that "[t]here's something comforting about… searching for the things that set Dad apart from everyone else." Elena Wolff, in "Paging Kafka's Elegist," hunts down the long-dead and long-forgotten friend of Franz Kafka, someone intimate with the great man, someone who could shed light on the author's early years. Don Gillmor's "In the Dying Hours of War: the Fate of Two Brothers" retraces the sad story of Gillmor's grandfather and his twin brother, who went off together to fight in the Great War, but only his grandfather returned. He, of course, was altered forever.

Personal memories have played an important part in a number of other powerful essays this year. Desmond Cole, in "The Skin I'm In," wants to know why he is treated consistently differently just because he is a man of colour, especially by the police. The author, in all of his days, should never have been a cause for alarm, and has had to behave that much better just because of his skin. In "The Unbelievers," Graeme Bayliss follows Muslims who have left their faith and explores the consequences on both sides of that decision. Carleigh Baker learns, in "Dinner with the Vittrekwas," what it means to travel naively to the Yukon without knowing what awaits, the wonders and dangers both. Krista Foss, in "Falling; Fallen," remembers a fall from her bike with her young daughter and pulls back the field of vision to include the fall of some of literature's most famous women—Emma Bovary, Anna Karenina and Edna Pontellier—and explores what the fall of women has come to mean over the past centuries. In "Living Susan Sontag's

Illness as Metaphor," Kenneth Sherman recalls what it meant for him to receive a diagnosis of advanced cancer and considers the extent to which you can rationalize such news, or keep it at a far enough remove to protect you from your fears.

On the far side of this spectrum are essays I would class as a purer form of journalism: non-fiction without reliance on the imagination, yet with the storyteller's gift still on full display. All are important, and all are riveting. Antanas Sileika gets us to consider other victims, not just the ones always in the news—in this case the victims of Communism—as outlined in "Fault Lines." These others, Sileika says, are also important. "Their memories are the memories of this country too." Richard Poplak tells the horrifying tale of "Dr. Shock," a sex offender acting as a psychiatrist first in apartheid-era South Africa, then in Canada, where finally, decades later, the law catches up with him. Fred Stenson enlightens us about big oil, in "Landowner Rights," and how corporations and government can have their way with property, any property they need or want. Michael Rowe talks about Internet culture in "Most Everyone is Mad Here," how our little bursts of temper and panic have created a culture of electronic squeaks and grunts and noises that might amount to little more than what they are. So is technology getting out of hand? You might find the answer in Wayne A. Hunt's "War and Peace in a Robotic Culture." Who exactly is going to be waging war and how? We should look to our artists to help us understand the trends because they remain the radar of our times and "perform a vital, but often unrecognized, democratic service."

What wisdom there is in this collection, what wit and charm and horror, what literature. Enjoy.

Joseph Kertes

Dinner with the Vittrekwas
Carleigh Baker

1.

WHAT THE HELL are we doing here, standing around like a bunch of chumps while Calder gets his money shot? Little guy with a big camera, following a bull moose down the beach. He doesn't need to get that close; surely the lens can zoom right in. Still, he looks pretty primal, stalking like a hunter for shots to fill in the spaces around the action. B-roll, he calls it. The moose does his moose thing, lopes down to the water and takes a drink.

Emma, the lead scientist on our team (and Calder's girlfriend), stands next to me, clucking and sighing about his proximity to the moose. She's right: it's risky to get too close, especially in September. Rutting season. The moose could decide he likes the looks of Calder and take a run at him. But the bull is swimming away now, soft brown nose raised comically above the water. Another reminder that the noble and harrowing Yukon landscape isn't particularly interested in us.

This isn't the first time I've wondered what I'm doing here, but it's too late to back out now. We are fourteen days into a 500-kilometre paddle through the Peel River Watershed. Six artists, two guides, two scientists, and a film crew. We began just off the Dempster Highway at the Ogilvie River and connected with

1

the Peel at its confluence with the Blackstone River. In a few days we'll cross the Arctic Circle and paddle eventually into the Northwest Territories, ending up in Fort McPherson, just upriver from the Mackenzie Delta on the Beaufort Sea. We're making a documentary, or I guess *Calder* is making the documentary and we're in it. As one of the artists, I'm supposed to be here to write, and maybe convince young urbanites like myself that they should pay attention to what's happening in the North.

At the moment, what's happening is that the Yukon government has decided to open the area to extensive oil and mining exploitation. The Peel Watershed spans nearly 68,000 square kilometres, and is one of the most striking mountain river ecosystems in North America. It's home to the Na-cho Nyak Dun, Tr'ondëk Hwëch'in, Vuntut Gwitchin, and Tetlit Gwich'in people. A legal battle is unfolding in the Supreme Court of Canada as we paddle, *First Nation of Na-cho Nyak Dun et al. v The Government of Yukon*. Most of us watched the trial in July, via live stream, or listened to the podcasts. Now we're meeting this land we're hoping to protect, via the kind of soft-sell artsy approach to environmentalism that's having a lot more success with millennials than the END OF THE WORLD IS NIGH narrative.

No one could mistake us for the epic historical explorers who preceded us. The drone camera is a dead giveaway. The film equipment—and there's a canoe full of it—runs on what precious solar power Calder can collect each day. We've had sun, but the camera crew misjudged the effects of the cold on their equipment—batteries drain in minutes, and the GPS on the drone camera doesn't work well this far north. At night, Calder sleeps with camera batteries in his sleeping bag.

It's not all pain. Sometimes it's pain freckled with pleasure. Yesterday we left the tall, stratified stone walls of Aberdeen Canyon to meet the cold sun in a wide open sky. Scrubby spruce on the tree line, golden-leafed willow bushes and silver driftwood on the shore. Smoke billowed in the distance, which caused a bit of a stir as people speculated whether it was a forest fire or campers. Turns out it was neither. Smoking Hill, our guide explained, is a coal seam that was hit by lightning ages ago and ignited; it's been holding at a slow burn ever since. There are mining claims all around us, but Smoking Hill is a surreal reminder of the minerals that make this place dangerously valuable. Last night the fire was my inspiration, lighting a Jack-o-lantern grin into the side of the hill. Under a sepia sky, I wrote poetry by the glow of my headlamp with only a hint of pretension. Such moments need to be stolen, subtracted from valuable sleep time, but they're worth it.

2.

We're looking for ourselves, right? That's what these transformative, Canadian journey stories are all about. Actually, most of the time, we're just looking at Calder to tell us where to stand, or the guides to tell us what to do. Hold this paddle, set up this tent, don't look directly at the camera. "This is going to look amazing," Calder says sometimes, and we have no choice but to believe him. We're friends, and when he asked me to come on the trip my trust in him made it easy. He's had this impermeable shell around him since, but I assume that just makes sense for the director. Protect the vision. If this was a controlled film set, he'd have his own trailer. Instead, he and Emma get their own space, while the rest of us bunk three to a tent, aligned like mackerel.

The artists are the stars of the show, or so we're told. Katie and Daniel are from Calgary; she paints and sketches, and he's known for some ambitious installation art. On one of our paddle days, he tells me about weeks spent fasting while painting the inside of a cave in Turkey. He did a similar project in a plexiglass box in downtown Calgary, gradually painting himself off from the world over a period of five days. Callan takes photographs, and Tony is a musician. They're both from Toronto. Tony brought a banjo and a violin on the trip, and occasionally there's enough time for him to play for us. His hands are usually so cold and cracked from the daily paddle—thirty to sixty kilometres a day—he can't play for long. The violin is particularly strange and spooky in the tundra, bringing the ravens out from the trees to investigate.

We all did a moving-water certification course in Whitehorse just days before the trip. Apart from that, Aurora, a glass artist and welder, has never paddled or camped at all. Ever. She's from Toronto as well, and a direct relative of Charles Darwin. She jokes that that little connection might get her through the trip. I'm more experienced than Aurora, and consider myself "outdoorsy," but I have never done anything this outdoorsy. Not even close. All the camping I've done before now looks positively wimpy.

My bloodline is Cree-Métis and Icelandic, which, between the Voyageurs and the Vikings, has led to joking about how well-suited I must be to the trip. But if Calder pointed his camera at me right now, I'd have nothing useful to say. Just whining. I'm sore. I'm cold. I imagine myself spending twenty days bitching into Calder's camera about how hard everything is. Opening the tent to a frost shower every morning for the first ten days. The daily endurance of a light, spitty rain, with nowhere to dry off, ever. Bundled up with our noses in journals and sketchbooks, trying to find the right synonym or brush stroke or camera angle to express cold. Chilly, cool, freezing, icy, snowy, wintry, frosty, frigid, gelid, bitter, biting, raw, bone-chilling, nippy. It's too cold to work. Since we're packed three to a tent, there's no chance to work in bed, even though the northern lights make much of the night as bright as dawn. My sleeping bag is rated for minus forty, but it's still not particularly warm.

I shiver myself to sleep most nights, thinking about where I fit in this landscape. A landscape I'm pretty pissed off at, honestly. One night, after sipping the drop of Scotch my body allows before a headache sets in, I proclaim that the best way to save the Peel would be to fly moneyed urbanites overhead and serve them drinks, because the river vistas are amazing. Actually being here is just misery.

3.

Just past the Arctic Circle, we find the bloody remnants of a moose at the river's edge. Bloated lungs and intestine, and a perfectly good pelt left behind for some reason. It's pretty fresh—birds of prey circle overhead. This is our first indicator of hunters on the river, of anyone besides us, actually. They could be local, or from some fly-in backcountry outfit. The whole scene makes me queasy. The others are all bent over, turning the pelt bloody side up and taking photos, poking the organs with a stick. "Don't puncture it," somebody says. "The smell will be deadly."

I'm annoyed by my squeamishness. I'm annoyed that I can't handle being cold and wet. What on earth convinced me that a diluted drop of Cree blood might serve me in the North? I'm an urbanite Métis wanna-be, raised white, and I have no place stomping through the North like a fool. I head down the beach a little. We're not supposed to get too far from the group, for safety reasons, but it's all treeless shoreline here. No sand, just polished rocks so round and colourful they look like decorative landscaping fill. I circle the group like a goldfish while they take a million photographs of the moose carcass. Then we all have to pose for more photos, as part of our crowdfunding obligations.

Calder's idea was to write personalized notes to our funders on a whiteboard and then take a photo (right at the Arctic Circle, folks!). But the dry erase markers, like the camera batteries, the GPS on the drone, and our tender extremities, don't work well in the cold. After a few tense minutes with everybody talking at once, it's decided that we'll take just one photo and Photoshop everyone's names in later. This gets us to snack time faster. Finally, a silver lining!

Snack time means a handful of cheese and one "fun-sized" chocolate bar each. "Fun-sized" means inadequate. Then it's back on the river. Today is particularly challenging—the rain has been constant since we woke and pulled ourselves out of tents we'd set up in thick dead grass that smelled like wet dog. The river here is thick and brown and sluggish. Paddling is the only time I get half warm, and the spray skirt that covers the canoe and cinches around my waist keeps heat in, so it's hard to leave. When lunchtime comes, we don't pull off the river to picnic, just tie the boats together and pass around some food. Pasta salad with a little bit of precious tuna broken into it, and some beans. Earlier in the trip there was lemon juice and dill, but overzealous chefs used more than they should. Now those preparing the meals are left with ground ginger and chili powder to get creative with.

It's not just the condiments that are getting low. Nobody wants to say it, but we're running out of food. I've heard the guides whispering to each other. Meal portions have been insufficient for days, and people are edgy. Most small talk is about what we'll eat when we get home. Our days on the river are now about marking off kilometres; we need to make 40-60 kilometres a day to make up for a slow start. At the end of each day, everybody is famished and can't help looming like vultures over whoever's preparing the food.

It's not just the quantity but also the quality of the food that's so depressing. Chocolate granola, while tasty, is a sugar crash waiting to happen. Grated cheese is a sad substitute for quality proteins. The meat is canned—canned tuna, canned ham, canned chicken—and there is precious little of it. Callan has a nut allergy so severe that nuts are banned. Seeds are okay. Bird food. I feel like a bird fairly often, a bird eating cheese. I remember Calder and one of the guides going out to buy groceries, telling us everything was taken care of. I don't want to admit it, but real concern is starting to grow inside me. If I had the Internet, I'd Google "northern adventure starvation," or "arrogant colonial explorers." We're not starving. But I'm so hungry I can't help musing about what starving would be like.

4.

The North has seen many ill-prepared travellers run out of provisions and lose their lives, and we're only a few days' paddle from the memorial site of one such group, known as The Lost Patrol. One of our guides has probably told the story to wide-eyed travellers a thousand times, but he agrees to do it again on camera for Calder when we arrive. They'll set him up with a lavalier mic and fuss over light and angles for a few minutes, the kind of Hollywood crap we're used to now.

On December 21, 1910, Francis Joseph Fitzgerald left Fort McPherson with three RCMP constables to lead the annual patrol to Dawson City. For some reason, he carried a lighter-than-usual supply of provisions on the 750-kilometre trek. There's speculation that he'd hoped to make record-breaking time. After wasting nine days trying to find the route across the Richardson Mountains in heavy snow, the patrol was forced to head back towards Fort McPherson. Records show the temperature dropped as low as minus sixty-one degrees that winter. When the food ran out, they began eating their dogs. Fitzgerald's diary was found at the site, his last entry dated the 5th of February. He reported that there were five dogs left, and the men were too weak to travel more than a short distance each day. Their bodies were found only a few kilometres from Fort McPherson. Three men died from exposure and starvation; one committed suicide.

The search party had been led by William Dempster, the namesake of the Dempster Highway, where we began our trip. Dempster had done the patrol successfully many times, but in March 1911 he must have set out with a heavy heart and some trepidation. The bodies of all four men were moved to Fort McPherson, where they were buried.

The annual patrols continued until 1921; measures were taken to ensure that the tragedy wasn't repeated. Cabins and regular caches were established along the trail in case of food shortages, and subsequent patrols always included an aboriginal guide. Our guide is not aboriginal, but he's very knowledgeable. Besides me, no one claims to have any aboriginal blood, and several members of the team haven't had much contact with First Nations people at all. Part of our plan involved hanging out with some of the folks who call the Peel home, but since we're so cold and short on food and behind schedule, it was decided we'd better make a beeline for Fort McPherson.

Fortunately, the Vittrekwas happened to meet us on the way.

5.

When we hear a boat approaching, our first outside contact in sixteen days, I have a little panic attack. I get this feeling that I might not be able to think of anything to say to somebody new, or that all the wrong words might come out. It probably makes more sense to be nervous about who the hell might be in the boat (maybe the same creeps who wasted the moose hide?) and what they want from us. But for whatever reason—exhaustion or the de-sensitizing effect of being surrounded by unseen predators like wolves and grizzlies—danger never crosses my mind.

"Shhhhh," somebody says, and we all listen, faces screwed up in concentration. We've been rafting for a bit, the boats loosely tied together so we float as one. It doesn't seem real, but suddenly there they are, bundled-up figures in a long, skinny flat-bottom river boat, less curious about us than we are about them. Grandmother and grandfather, it turns out, Ernest and Alice. Alice's sister Margaret, and Kirk, an adopted son. They have guns. Looking for moose, they tell us. With unnaturally loud voices, we trip over each other to tell them about the carcass, wondering aloud why the pelt would have been left behind. Ernest and Alice say little about it, so the topic is dropped.

"Late in the season for canoe trips," Ernest says finally.

I cast a glance at Calder. So. Even the locals think it's late for us to be here. The women are wearing serious Arctic parkas, no messing around. Kirk is a typical teenager, underdressed, jacket unzipped. Ernest has a baseball hat and a down jacket; he's grizzled and missing teeth. He mumbles a little when he talks, so Alice repeats what he says. She is tiny, tough-looking, probably a few years younger than he is. She's looking us over with a grandmother's concern. Her brow creases when somebody makes a joke about not having enough to eat.

"Why don't you have enough to eat?" Her voice is sharp.

Meek backpedaling: we *kind of* have enough to eat, we're not *that* cold, we'll be okay.

"Well, you better head to our camp," Ernest says. "It's just down the way." When no one responds, Alice tells us they've got coffee and sugar. Since we ran out of both days ago, it's a mind-blowing thought. "There's a fire, and an outhouse," Alice adds. No ice-cold hole in the ground? Also mind-blowing.

They leave us to hunt farther up river. At the promise of hot drinks and toilets, we practically fly down river to their camp. A collection of old mattresses and lumber at beach level leaves no doubt that we've arrived. I use the term "beach" loosely; it's more like shin-deep mud. We pull our boats up as far as possible and I bound up the stairs to Ernest and Alice's camp. The proud outhouse stands not far from a slack-roofed shack, and a blue tarp we saw from the water covers the outdoor common area. There's a hearth, and a table covered with coffee fixings. Beyond is the main cabin, simple and weathered, with a small deck out front. Piles of split wood are everywhere, and the whole property looks over the Peel. It's humble, but we might as well be on a five-star cruise ship overlooking the Mayan Riviera.

Despite having been invited to make ourselves at home, Calder hesitates. There's some question whether we'll stay, even whether the invitation was really an invitation. Much to my frustration, I'm told to wait on the fire, wait on the coffee. "But, we've been invited," I bleat. Not accepting their invitation feels to me rude at best and, at worst, something like paternalism—the politest of discriminatory behaviours. Maybe my fellow travellers have decided the Vittrekwas don't have enough to share? Watching the others look around the camp with eyebrows raised, this is what I suspect. But then who the hell am I, a Métis wanna-be, to speak up for the Vittrekwas?

When our hosts return, we're still standing on the beach with a big question mark over our heads. I take the lead for once, running up to the boat and accepting an armful of Ernest's gear to take up to camp. One by one, uncertainly, my campmates follow.

"Why didn't you start the fire?" Alice says. Nobody answers.

Swept up in the current of our hosts, things happen. The fire gets made, coffee gets brewed in giant pots. Cups are distributed, and I fill mine first. Alice leads us into the sway-roofed shack, where a wood stove throws a heat none of us has experienced in weeks. She says we can sleep there for the night. The idea is intoxicating. Food is produced at such a rate that we can barely keep up. Cookies and biscuits; bannock with butter and jam; dried fish and candies and, of course, bottomless coffee. After dark, wieners are brought out to roast, mustard and ketchup passed around. For our part, we make fudge, which is nibbled on delicately by Margaret and Alice. Kirk has not shown himself since they pulled up in the boat. "He's shy," Alice says simply.

With the firelight dancing between us, Alice, having correctly identified me as the oldest female in the group, pulls me aside.

"Why didn't you have enough food?" she asks sternly.

"You're asking the wrong person," I start, raising my voice comically to implicate those who were in charge of food, but I can see she is genuinely concerned. It's not the time for jokes.

"Why didn't you call ahead, ask us for help?" By "us," she means everyone at Fort McPherson, a town full of experts in Northern travel.

"I don't know, Alice. I was told there would be enough food, and I trusted the people in charge."

"What do any of you know about being up here?" she says, with compassion cutting her ire.

I could tell her that our guide is a local, and that Calder's done plenty of tripping—the same script I'd been reading to myself for days now.

"Nothing," I answer finally. "We were getting into trouble. We should have asked for help."

It feels good saying this. Fault is irrelevant at this point, as is anger. More exhausting emotion, and we need all the strength we can get. She nods, lower lip protruding like a vindicated child. And then, without another word, she resumes her grandmother role.

That night, I can tell by the energy in the cabin that few of us actually sleep. The coffee didn't help. But there's also the feeling of wanting to enjoy every moment of warmth and comfort. In the morning, most people confirm my suspicion. They didn't sleep and couldn't care less. The sensation of being nurtured, after feeling so deprived, is gigantic, overwhelming. In less than twenty-four hours, our mood has changed from grim acceptance to celebration and optimism. I have nothing sardonic to say about it.

For breakfast, it's oatmeal and boiled eggs and dried fish. Then the Vittrekwas load us up with coffee and more than enough supplies to keep us fed until the end of the trip. We take our time packing and cleaning the shack, savouring every moment inside. Calder does an interview with Ernest, Alice, and Margaret. Callan takes some photos. One of the scientists sharpens Ernest's axes, then chops and stacks wood for an hour. Nobody wants to leave. When we finally do, we're happy, full, and—though nobody mentions it—foolishly guilty of continuing in the tradition of unprepared white explorers in the North.

Last night, Ernest told us that when a successful moose hunt comes home to Fort McPherson, it's radioed in and any surplus is shared. That's how community works. That's how northern river culture works. And it makes room for outsiders—even stupid, well-intentioned tourists, self-anointed protectors of the Peel, become beneficiaries of this kindness.

"Just make sure you tell people about the Peel," Alice says in my ear when I hug her goodbye.

Back on the mighty, muddy Peel, the cold continues, the rain continues. Now, instead of talking about what we're going to eat when we get off the river for good, we talk about Ernest and Alice. When we reach the Lost Patrol memorial, a weathered wood pyramid with a plaque on it, the Vittrekwas pass us in their boat, headed home for the season. We wave. Three days away, in Fort McPherson, they'll welcome us again.

The Unbelievers
Graeme Bayliss

KIRAN OPAL SAT in a quiet corner of the house, holding a slice of pizza and waiting to explode. A few minutes earlier, the thirteen-year-old had gone from hanging out with friends at a birthday party to making the most important decision of her life: cheese or pepperoni?

She knew which was the right choice. She knew that God was watching. But the smell was overpowering. She reached for the tantalizing mass of meat and cheese and took a bite. Then she skulked away, ashamed and afraid of what might happen next. Pork was *haram*—forbidden—but Opal had eaten it anyway. And worse still, she had liked it. She knew the grisly punishments that God visited upon sinners: the melting skin, the lightning bolts, the garments of fire. She did not want her friends to witness the divine repercussions that she would now surely face.

So she sat and awaited God's wrath. But God's wrath never came: not after she rejoined her friends a few minutes later, nor in the days and weeks that followed. "I remember the fear," says Opal, now thirty-seven and living in Toronto's west end. "I'm so far away from it, but I still remember that gut fear."

Six years after that first act of defiance, Opal left Islam for good. She had spent her teenage years trying to appease her parents by playing the role of the devout Muslim, but she could not keep up the act. "I always had to do more and more to prove myself to them," she says. "And I felt worse and worse." She began to shirk her religious duties, praying less often and making up excuses not to go to mosque. Even when she stopped practising her religion altogether, the terror she had felt at the birthday party remained. It took about seven more years before she got over her vestigial fear of hell.

The decision to leave Islam is a serious one, usually made after protracted struggles with doubt, shame and fear. Apostasy is considered the greatest sin a Muslim can commit. According to the Library of Congress, it is a prosecutable offence in twenty-three countries—in nine it can be punishable by death. But apostasy is difficult not only for Muslims living in countries where religion is law. Even in Canada, the freedom to disbelieve can be circumscribed by menacing social pressures. Apostates, known as *murtads* or *kafirs* in Islam, are often ostracized by their communities and disowned by their families, causing emotional and financial distress.

But in recent years, some apostates have discovered that they do not have to face their isolation alone. In 2013, Opal co-founded Ex-Muslims of North America, or EXMNA, a non-profit that offers safe spaces for former believers to meet and share their experiences through monthly meetings and robust online support. In three years, the organization has spread to eighteen North American cities, boasting hundreds of members—the majority of whom have not "come out" as non-believers to their friends or family. For these people, EXMNA is the only support they have.

As a teenager, Sadaf Ali never considered leaving Islam. The concept simply did not occur to her. "Something my mother used to tell me growing up was that you can't *not* be a Muslim," she says. "Your father is Muslim, your grandfather is Muslim and his father before that. It's just something you can't leave."

In fact, Ali could not do much of anything without ostensibly Koran-backed interference from her parents. They forced her to work at their restaurant for less than minimum wage. They controlled her hours, leaving her no free time on weekends and crippling her social life. She felt alone. Her parents did not support her desire to go to university, and although they eventually relented, they made sure she stayed near home and under close watch; while attending the University of Toronto, she was forced to live in nearby Mississauga with her uncle and grandmother. Through everything, her parents cited Islam as justification.

At eighteen, just a few months into her first year of university, Ali was struggling with depression and anxiety, conditions exacerbated by years of family conflict. She fantasized about dropping out of school and volunteering in Tunisia, of learning to speak French and disappearing into a world thousands of kilometres from home. She had few people to speak with, but one cousin offered some advice: take your fears and your anxieties, write them down on a piece of paper and put them in the ground. Coming home late from school one night, Ali waited for her bus driver to pull away from her apartment building; then she dropped to her knees and began to dig at the wintry earth with her bare hands. In the shallow hole, Ali placed a slip of paper admitting that she was not sure whether she believed in God anymore—something she had never been able to say aloud. Later, in her bedroom, she faced Mecca and asked why she had been made to feel so alone. What had she done to deserve her broken childhood? "And that's when I realized I was talking to myself," Ali recalls. "No one is listening to me. No one gives a shit about me. There isn't some man in the sky who has this fate for me."

It took Ali three years to come out as an atheist to her parents. They took it badly, devastated by the thought that their daughter might face an eternity in hell. And although Ali avoided going home in the aftermath, she could not escape her family. Her parents phoned constantly. Her brother called too, angry that Ali had renounced her faith and left their mother in tears. "He told me to keep my opinions and my beliefs to myself," Ali says. Her father once sent her a Shia book, along with a handwritten note imploring her to pray for salvation. In the immediate aftermath, some members of her extended family refused to speak with her, including cousins with whom she was close. "They think that because I've left religion and don't agree with their cultural practices that I'm suddenly a bad person," she says. "They don't think that I have any morals."

One day in 2011, while browsing Reddit, Ali came across the community "Exmuslim," which today has about ten thousand subscribers. Suddenly there was a name for her—an identity she had always been denied. She began to chat with some of the other members, adopting their peculiar argot—"ex-Moose" for ex-Muslim; "Big Mo'" for Muhammad; and "in the closet" and "coming out," appropriated from the vernacular of the LGBTQ movement. Through this forum, Ali spoke with two other apostates from Toronto, Opal and then twenty-five-year-old Nas Ishmael, about leaving Islam and the isolation she felt. They decided to meet up in person.

Just six people attended that awkward session in March 2012, at an oyster bar in Toronto's Koreatown. "We were all just sitting around like, 'So, here we are,'" says Ishmael, who today is the media-relations director of EXMNA. Then someone told a blasphemous joke ("We make a lot of jokes about bacon," Ishmael explains), and another passed around an old student ID card revealing the Spanish moss of a beard that once hung from his chin. The ice was broken. The meeting was nothing revolutionary, but it was liberating for everyone to be able to speak openly about their apostasy.

The group began to hold monthly sessions, which steadily grew over the next year and a half (today it is not uncommon for thirty or more members to attend a meeting). Through the ex-Muslim forum, Ali and Ishmael discovered that a number of apostates were holding similar events in Washington, DC. Americans Muhammad Syed and Sarah Haider reached out to the Toronto group to discuss forming a larger umbrella organization for ex-Muslim support. "It seemed like there was a real need for it," Syed recalls. With a formal structure, the group could lend legitimacy to the notion that there is such a thing as life—and community—without Islam. EXMNA was formed.

Since the organization was established in September 2013, it has expanded rapidly, with groups in Houston, Philadelphia, Vancouver and Winnipeg, among others. In September 2015, the organization's eighteenth branch sprouted in Columbus, Ohio. There are now about five hundred members across North America, with more than one hundred in the Toronto chapter alone. The group even offers online meet-ups so that ex-Muslims in more remote settings can still be a part of the community.

Today, organizing events remains EXMNA's core function, although it also publishes an online magazine called the Ex-Muslim and is hoping to launch a podcast that would give closeted apostates the chance to tell their personal stories anonymously. Board members are volunteers, and although EXMNA is a charitable non-profit in the United States, donations can be hard to come by; members attending atheist and freethinking conferences often pay travel expenses out of pocket. The organization has recently involved itself in more international work, offering advice to apostates abroad and even connecting them with EXMNA members in their home countries (often international students who joined while studying in Canada or the US). For now, though, the group is primarily focused on creating communities at home. "We barely have the capacity to do what we're doing in North America," Syed says. "So we do what we can, when we can."

"You do not deserve to be on Allah's earth." Sarah Haider looked at the anonymous message; it was her first death threat. "Tell me where you are and I will burn you and every other *kafir* for going against the will of Allah and spreading lies. It must be done. Watch your back."

Security has been a concern for EXMNA since its inception. This letter—the first of many the organization has since received—went on to say that ex-Muslims deserved to have acid thrown at their mothers' faces for having raised children like them. While Haider says that few of the threats that members receive are credible, it can be difficult to distinguish garden-variety internet vitriol from genuine danger.

And it is not only anonymous online commenters who leave members worried. In the summer of 2014, Haider was preparing to deliver a speech on Islam and women's rights at the Pennsylvania State Atheist/Humanist Conference. She and Syed recall receiving an email from a Muslim scholar who wanted to debate Haider on her understanding of the religion (in his view, of course, her understanding was all wrong). The man never actually addressed Haider in his email; instead he requested to debate her through Syed, as if he were seeking a parent's permission to speak with a child. That the man would not condescend to address a woman smacked of fundamentalism to both recipients and made them wary. Haider politely declined—but the man bought a ticket and showed up anyway. "Nothing about that is particularly scary on its own," Haider says. "It's only in the ex-Muslim context that it becomes a scary thing to do." She says that religious fervour can turn into violence. "It's hard to know," Haider continues, "if the person is unhinged and feels it's their religious duty to take you down. It's not unprecedented for that kind of thing to happen."

At the conference, the man aggressively harangued his unwilling adversary, rejecting the notion that the abuse of women's rights was directly tied to religion in Muslim-majority countries. He did not threaten anyone, but Haider recalls that he became increasingly hostile as he held the floor. Afterwards, a handful of audience members offered to escort Haider to her hotel room and anywhere else she might need to go, which she accepted. "Everyone just had this panicked look on their face," she says, "because they were all thinking the same thing."

Events like these are why the Toronto and Washington ex-Muslim groups independently devised security procedures to screen potential members, which were later refined when EXMNA formed. The founders will not disclose exactly what these procedures entail, only that they involve a volunteer, often using a fake name, getting to know a prospective member over Skype and attempting to determine whether the prospect is, in fact, an ex-Muslim. Once the group is satisfied that its criteria have been met—which can sometimes take several interviews and a background check—they will provide the prospect with the time and location of their local chapter's next meeting.

There have been close calls in the past. Syed says that one Muslim man tried to cause trouble with the then-nascent Washington chapter in 2012. The prospect managed to get his screener's real name and phone number, which he then posted to social media, describing the activities of the ex-Muslim group to a number of Islamist organizations and vaguely but ominously insisting that something needed to be done about them. "That experience really shook us," Syed says, adding that as EXMNA grows, it will need to be even more vigilant. (It will also need to be more efficient: the waiting list to join is dozens of names long, a backlog that tends to worsen during holidays such as Ramadan, when closeted ex-Muslim screeners are surrounded by practising family and friends.)

The screening process is, of course, about ensuring the safety of EXMNA's members, although not only from the threat of violence. A meet-up is meant to be a safe space in the more abstract sense, too: a place where apostates can discuss their issues without feeling judged or unduly exposed. For that reason, Ishmael says, the group does not allow ex-Muslims who have left Islam for another faith to attend meetings. "When you leave Islam for another religion, you have the support system of that religion," he explains. "When you leave Islam for no other religion, where do you go? That's the space we offer."

The organization also prohibits practising Muslims who are questioning their faith. This, too, is for the purpose of maintaining a safe space. But some critics argue the policy results in little more than preaching to the choir. Sheima Benembarek* is a self-described moderate Muslim from Morocco who works as an editor for the United Church Observer. She says that banning questioning Muslims from meet-ups creates a kind of echo chamber, a space where everybody agrees with everybody else, fostering the notion that their position is the only correct one—a lot like the mosques they decry. "Anybody that's genuinely interested in opening their parameters and bettering themselves as a person isn't going to be that closed off," she says.

Still, for nearly all members, absolute discretion is a prerequisite to participation in meetings. Some have not revealed their apostasy to their families; others have concerns for their personal security. Irqa Khan† is a member of EXMNA's Toronto chapter. She has not come out as a non-believer to her parents. Born in Pakistan and raised in the US, Khan experienced constant domestic violence growing up. "My mom has a lot of dental issues because of the number of times her teeth have been knocked out," she says. At five, Khan borrowed a boy's bike; for the transgression, her father picked her up and shook her until she passed out. She hopes that she will never have to tell her parents about her apostasy. Meanwhile, a Somali member, who asked not to be identified because he comes from a small fundamentalist community in Ontario, notes that since he has family in Yemen, Somalia and Kenya, his apostasy could result in trouble abroad. "If I go to any of those countries," he says, "I could be killed."

EXMNAS founders have been disheartened by the perception, both of conservative Muslims and of secular liberals, that their group is anti-Muslim. Benembarek is among those who hold that view. "I don't buy that they're these reasonable, rational intellectuals who don't actually have any anger toward anybody." Benembarek adds that their "juvenile" vernacular—those words that helped Sadaf Ali connect to others like her online—betrays their Islamophobia. Organizations like EXMNA have also faced criticism from prominent academics, including Deepa Kumar, a professor of media studies at Rutgers University and the author of the 2012 book *Islamophobia and the Politics of Empire*. At a public lecture this June on Islamophobia, Kumar referred to ex-Muslims as "native informants"—comparing adults determining their own beliefs to quislings collaborating with their colonial oppressors.

Yet EXMNA's organizers insist they harbour no ill feelings toward Muslims who practise their faith within the confines of Western values such as equality and universal rights; it is only Muslims who transgress those values in the name of religion that they oppose. EXMNA members also say that calling their organization Islamophobic is particularly vexing: not only does it muzzle critics of the religion with implications of racism, but for ex-Muslims, it does not even make sense. "Islamophobia means an irrational fear of Islam, right?" Ishmael says. "As apostates, we have a very rational fear."

Ishmael acknowledges that anti-Muslim bigotry exists and

that it should be combated, but he says that to use the term Islamophobia to encompass that bigotry, as well as to shield the religion from criticism, is unfair to every Muslim who has ever been discriminated against, including just about every member of the ex-Muslim community. "I've been told to go back to my country," says Ali, who left EXMNA in early 2015 when her involvement began to take up more time than she could afford. "I know what it's like to experience racism. But a lot of people don't understand that. We're not turning against anyone, we're not turning against our people..."

Ishmael interjects: "All we want is just to exist."

Bilal Azad[†] remembers the day he told the Toronto EXMNA chapter that he had come out to his family. "I felt like a superhero," he says. Azad explains that he originally planned to tell his mother and father about his apostasy after he turned twenty-five. Instead, his experience with EXMNA encouraged him to do so just four months after he attended his first meeting, when he was twenty. "My biggest fear was that if I came out to my family, I wouldn't have anyone," he says. He quips that while he now gets disowned every weekend by his mercurial parents, thanks to EXMNA, he is never without family. Still, there are parts of Islam that Azad misses.

The ritualistic elements of religion are part of what makes believers feel connected to something bigger than themselves. And, imposed or not, the sense of community and identity that Islam engenders through those rituals can be difficult for ex-Muslims to give up.

Many women, such as Khan, continue to wear their hijabs ("I still feel naked without it," she explains). Some ex-Muslims still enter the bathroom leading with their left foot, as scripture dictates. Others have trouble giving up prayer. Azad continued to pray for years after leaving Islam, during a period in which he identified as a deist. "I truly believed that prayer was a form of meditation," he says. "Regardless of whether there's a God or not, the concept of prayer and the action of praying were still beneficial to me."

But rituals, traditions and the communities that form around them can exist in secular life, too, and EXMNA is working to create them. Members who come out to their relatives often find that they miss the familial conviviality of events such as Eid, the feast that marks the end of Ramadan. But the group has that covered; in 2014, it organized Haramadan (playing on the Arabic for "forbidden"), giving apostates who have become distant from their families the chance to celebrate with friends instead. It includes a new tradition called Secret *Shaitan*—that is, Secret Satan—in which members exchange gifts based on a given theme. It may not entirely account for lost family time, but it is something.

Other former Muslims create rituals for themselves. Irqa Khan gave up on Islam during Ramadan, as she was fasting for forgiveness and fighting back hunger pangs. One day, she noticed that a co-worker had abandoned a carton of French fries on his office table. In that moment, Khan knew that she was done with her religion. "I looked up, and I'm like, *You know what, screw this bullshit.* And I ate all his fries." Today, the dish holds a particular significance for her: whenever EXMNA meets at a bar, she orders fries—and none of the other members know why. "Those have become the love of my life," she says, laughing, "because they were there for me."

Trade-offs are a big part of ex-Muslim life: family for new friends; Eid for Haramadan; faith for French fries. But for EXMNA members, at least, the benefits outweigh the costs. "I have freedom of thought, and that's been worth more than anything," Khan says. "Not to be afraid of the things I think anymore."

Benembarek is a former colleague of the author.
†*Name has been changed to protect privacy.*

The Skin I'm In
Desmond Cole

THE SUMMER I was nine, my teenage cousin Sana came from England to visit my family in Oshawa. He was tall, handsome and obnoxious, the kind of guy who could palm a basketball like Michael Jordan. I was his shadow during his visit, totally in awe of his confidence—he was always saying something clever to knock me off balance.

One day, we took Sana and his parents on a road trip to Niagara Falls. Just past St. Catharines, Sana tossed a dirty tissue out the window. Within seconds, we heard a siren: a cop had been driving behind us, and he immediately pulled us onto the shoulder. A hush came over the car as the stocky officer strode up to the window and asked my dad if he knew why we'd been stopped. "Yes," my father answered, his voice shaky, like a child in the principal's office. My dad isn't a big man, but he always cut an imposing figure in our household. This was the first time I realized he could be afraid of something. "He's going to pick it up right now," he assured the officer nervously, as Sana exited the car to retrieve the garbage. The cop seemed casually uninterested, but everyone in the car thrummed with tension, as if they were bracing for something catastrophic. After Sana returned, the officer let us go. We drove off, overcome with silence until my father finally exploded. "You realize everyone in this car is black, right?" he thundered at Sana. "Yes, Uncle," Sana whispered, his head down and shoulders slumped. That afternoon, my imposing father and cocky cousin had trembled in fear over a discarded Kleenex.

My parents immigrated to Canada from Freetown, Sierra Leone, in the mid-1970s. I was born in Red Deer, Alberta, and soon after, we moved to Oshawa, where my father was a mental health nurse and my mother a registered nurse who worked with the elderly. Throughout my childhood, my parents were constantly lecturing me about respecting authority, working hard and preserving our family's good name. They made it clear that although I was the same as my white peers, I would have to try harder and achieve more just to keep up. I tried to ignore what they said about my race, mostly because it seemed too cruel to be true.

In high school, I threw myself into extra-curricular activities— student council, choir, tennis, soccer, fundraising drives for local charities—and I graduated valedictorian of my class. Despite my misgivings about my parents' advice, I was proud to be living up to their expectations. In 2001, I earned admission to Queen's University. I was enticed by the isolated, scenic campus—it looked exactly like the universities I'd seen in movies, with stately buildings and waterfront views straight out of *Dead Poets Society*. When I told my older sister, who was studying sociology at Western, she furrowed her brow. "It's so *white*," she bristled. That didn't matter much to me: Oshawa was just as white as Kingston, and I was used to being the only black kid in the room. I wasn't going to let my race dictate my future.

At Queen's, I was one of about 80 black undergrads out of 16,000. In second year, when I moved into the student village, I started noticing cops following me in my car. At first, I thought I was being paranoid—I began taking different roads to confirm my suspicions. No matter which route I took, there was usually a police cruiser in my rear-view mirror. Once I felt confident I was being followed, I became convinced that if I went home, the police would know where I lived and begin following me there too. I'd drive around aimlessly, taking streets I didn't know.

I had my first face-to-face interaction with the Kingston police a few months into second year, when I was walking my friend Sara, a white woman, back to her house after a party. An officer stopped us, then turned his back to me and addressed Sara directly. "Miss, do you need assistance?" he asked her. Sara was stunned into silence. "No," she said twice—once to the officer, and once to reassure herself that everything was all right. As he walked away, we were both too shaken to discuss what had happened, but in the following days we recounted the incident many times over, as if grasping to remember if it had really occurred. The fact that my mere presence could cause an armed stranger to feel threatened on Sara's behalf shocked me at first, but shock quickly gave way to bitterness and anger.

As my encounters with police became more frequent, I began to see every uniformed officer as a threat. The cops stopped me anywhere they saw me, particularly at night. Once, as I was walking through the laneway behind my neighbourhood pizza parlour, two officers crept up on me in their cruiser. "Don't move," I whispered to myself, struggling to stay calm as they got out of their vehicle. When they asked me for identification, I told them it was in my pocket before daring to reach for my wallet. If they thought I had a weapon, I was convinced that I'd end up being beaten, or worse. I stood in the glare of the headlights, trying to imagine how I might call out for help if they attacked me. They left me standing for about 10 minutes before one of them—a white man who didn't look much older than me—approached to return my identification. I summoned the courage to ask why he was doing this. "There's been some suspicious activity in the area," he said, shrugging his shoulders. Then he said I could go. Another time, an officer stopped me as I was walking home from a movie. When I told him I wasn't carrying ID, he twisted his face in disbelief. "What do you mean?" he asked. "Sir, it's important that you always carry identification," he said, as if he was imparting friendly advice. Everywhere I went, he was saying, I should be prepared to prove I wasn't a criminal, even though I later learned I was under no legal obligation to carry ID. When I told my white friends about these encounters with police, they'd often respond with skepticism and dismissal, or with a barrage of questions that made me doubt my own sanity. "But what were you doing?" they'd badger, as if I'd withheld some key part of the story that would justify the cops' behaviour.

When I was 22, I decided to move to Toronto. We'd visited often when I was a kid, driving into the city for festivals and fish markets and dinners with other families from Sierra Leone. In Toronto, I thought I could escape bigotry and profiling, and just blend into the crowd. By then, I had been stopped, questioned and followed by the police so many times I began to expect it. In Toronto, I saw diversity in the streets, in shops, on public transit. The idea that I might be singled out because of my race seemed ludicrous. My illusions were shattered immediately.

My skin is the deep brown of a well-worn penny. My eyes are the same shade as my complexion, but they light up amber in the sun, like a glass of whiskey. On a good day, I like the way I look. At other times, particularly when people point out how dark I am, I want to slip through a crack in the ground and disappear. White people often go out of their way to say they don't see colour when they look at me—in those moments, I'm tempted to recommend an optometrist. I know they're just expressing a desire for equality, but I don't want to be erased in the process. When I walk down the street, I find myself imagining that strangers view me with suspicion and fear. This phenomenon is what the African-American writer and activist W.E.B. Du Bois described as "double-consciousness": how blacks experience reality through their own eyes and through the eyes of a society that prejudges them.

I hate it when people ask me where I'm from, because my answer is often followed by, "But where are you *really* from?" When they ask that question, it's as though they're implying I don't belong here. The black diaspora has rippled across Toronto: Somalis congregate in Rexdale, Jamaicans in Keelesdale, North Africans in Parkdale. We make up 8.5 per cent of the city's population, but the very notion of a black Torontonian conflates hundreds of different languages, histories, traditions and stories. It could mean dark-skinned people who were born here or elsewhere, who might speak Arabic or Patois or Portuguese, whose ancestors may have come from anywhere in the world. In the National Household Survey, the term "black" is the only classification that identifies a skin colour rather than a nation or region.

There's this idea that Toronto is becoming a post-racial city, a multicultural utopia where the colour of your skin has no bearing on your prospects. That kind of thinking is ridiculously naïve in a city and country where racism contributes to a self-perpetuating cycle of criminalization and imprisonment. Areas where black people live are heavily policed in the name of crime prevention, which opens up everyone in that neighbourhood to disproportionate scrutiny. We account for 9.3 per cent of Canadian prisoners, even though we only make up 2.9 per cent of the populace at large. And anecdotal evidence suggests that more and more people under arrest are pleading guilty to avoid pretrial detention—which means they're more likely to end up with a criminal record. Black people are also more frequently placed in maximum-security institutions, even if the justice system rates us as unlikely to be violent or to reoffend: between 2009 and 2013, 15 per cent of black male inmates were assigned to maximum-security, compared to 10 per cent overall. If we're always presumed guilty, and if we receive harsher punishments for the same crimes, then it's no surprise that many of us end up in poverty, dropping out of school and reoffending.

About a decade ago, the Toronto Police Service established carding, a controversial practice that disproportionately targets young black men and documents our activities across the city. According to police parlance, it's a voluntary interaction with people who are not suspected of a crime. Cops stop us on the street, demand identification, and catalogue our race, height, weight and eye colour. Until early this year, these fill-in-the-blanks forms—known as Field Information Reports—also had slots to identify a civilian as a "gang member" or "associate"; to record a person's body markings, facial hair and cellphone number; and, for minors, to indicate whether their parents were divorced or separated. All that information lives in a top-secret database, ostensibly in the interest of public safety, but the police have never provided any evidence to show how carding reduces or solves crime. They've also failed to justify carding's excessive focus on black men. The *Toronto Star* crunched the numbers and found that in 2013, 25 per cent of people carded were black. At that time, I was 17 times more likely than a white person to be carded in Toronto's downtown core.

In late March, the TPS revamped their carding policy, announcing with much self-congratulatory back-slapping that they'd rebranded the FIR cards as "community engagement reports," implemented a plan for racial sensitivity training and eliminated carding quotas for officers. But when you look at the fine print, it's clear that little has changed. Under their new procedures, police do not have to inform civilians that a carding interaction is voluntary, that they can walk away at any time. Cops won't be required to tell civilians why they are being stopped, and their internal justifications for a stop are so broad they might as well not exist. Worst of all, the database where police have been storing this information will still be used.

In a recent report to the Toronto Police Services Board, residents in 31 Division, which includes several low-income and racialized neighbourhoods in northwest Toronto, were candid about their views of police. Many said our cops disrespect them, stop them without cause and promote a climate of constant surveillance in their neighbourhoods. Some respondents to the TPSB survey said they now avoid certain areas within their own neighbourhoods for fear of encountering police. Black respondents were most likely to report that police treated them disrespectfully, intimidated them or said they fit the description of a criminal suspect. "Police are supposed to serve and protect, but it always feels like a battle between us and them," one survey participant said.

I have been stopped, if not always carded, at least 50 times by the police in Toronto, Kingston and across southern Ontario. By now, I expect it could happen in any neighbourhood, day or night, whether I am alone or with friends. These interactions don't scare me anymore. They make me angry. Because of that unwanted scrutiny, that discriminatory surveillance, I'm a prisoner in my own city.

When I arrived in Toronto in 2004, I had no idea what I wanted to do other than escape my suburban hometown and the bigotry I'd faced in Kingston. For the first few months, I crashed with my childhood friend Matthew at his grandfather's East York home. I didn't have much money, so I spent a lot of time wandering downtown, sitting in parks or coffee shops, marvelling at the diversity I saw on the streets. I was enjoying an anonymity I had never experienced before. One night I set out, journal in hand, to find somewhere to write. Less than a minute into my stroll, a police cruiser stopped me on Holborne Avenue, near Woodbine and Cosburn.

"How are you doing this evening?" one of the two officers asked from the car. By now I was familiar with this routine. I'd been stopped a dozen times in Kingston and followed so frequently I'd lost count. "I'm okay," I replied, trying to stay calm. "What are you doing?" the officer continued. "Walking," I said with a glare. When he asked me if I lived around there, I replied that I didn't have to disclose that information. My mouth was dry and my heart was racing—I didn't usually refuse police requests during confrontations, but my frustration had got the better of me. "Could you tell me what street we're on right now?" the cop asked. I was quaking with rage at this unsolicited game of 20 questions. "Anyone can tell you that," I shot back, trying not to raise my voice. "There's a street sign right in front of you."

My parents would have been furious—they'd always taught me to politely answer any questions I was asked. The police had the upper hand. But I'd lost patience. I demanded to know why I was being stopped. "We've had some break-and-enters in this area recently," the officer replied, as if that explained everything. "Well, unless you think I'm the culprit, I have the right to walk in peace." The officer seemed taken aback. He quickly wished me good night, and they drove off. I was so shaken I could have sat down and cried, but I realized the street I was living on was no longer a safe place to stand at night. I walked briskly to the Danforth, where I escaped into a bar.

After bouncing all over the city trying to find work, I eventually got a job at a drop-in centre for homeless youth at Queen and Spadina. As I settled into my life in Toronto, unwanted attention followed me everywhere I went. That year was 2005, the Summer of the Gun, when a streak of Toronto murders made headlines around the country. Most of the shooting victims and suspects were young black men, many of them alleged gang members, and the surge of violence stoked a culture of racial anxiety. I read about these shootings with sadness, but also with fear that people were reflexively associating me with gun crimes. If someone ignored me when I asked for directions on the street, or left the seat next to me vacant on the streetcar, I wondered if they were afraid of me.

In Kingston, I was used to women crossing the street when they saw me approaching, but until I moved to Toronto, I'd never seen them run. One night, I stepped off a bus on Dufferin Street at the same time as a young woman in her 20s. She took a couple of steps, looked over her shoulder at me, and tore into a full sprint. I resisted the urge to call out in my own defence. In 2006, I ran for Toronto city council in Trinity-Spadina. As I canvassed houses along Bathurst Street, a teenage girl opened the door, took one look at me, and bolted down the hallway. She didn't even close the door. When her mother appeared a moment later and apologized, I couldn't tell which of us was more embarrassed.

That same year, I was denied entry to a popular bar on College Street. The bouncer told me I couldn't come in with the shoes I had on, a pair of sneakers that resembled those of countless other guys in the queue. Fuming, I began to object, but I quickly realized that a black guy causing a scene at a nightclub was unlikely to attract much sympathy. I didn't want to embarrass the half-dozen friends I'd come with. We left quietly, and I've never gone back.

Shortly after my (unsuccessful) election campaign, I went to a downtown pub to watch hockey with some friends and my girlfriend at the time, a white child-care worker named Heather. The Leafs won, and the place turned into a party. Heather and I were dancing, drinking and having a great time. On my way back from the washroom, two bouncers stopped me and said I had to leave. "We just can't have that kind of stuff around here," one of them informed me. I asked what "stuff" he meant, but he and his partner insisted I had to go. They followed closely behind me as I went back upstairs to inform Heather and my friends that I was being kicked out. My friends seemed confused and surprised, but none made a fuss or questioned the bouncers who stood behind me. People stopped dancing to see what was going on and, recognizing that security was involved, kept their distance. I tried not to make eye contact with anyone as the guards escorted me out of the bar.

I have come to accept that some people will respond to me with fear or suspicion—no matter how irrational it may seem. After years of needless police scrutiny, I've developed habits to check my own behaviour. I no longer walk through upscale clothing stores like Holt Renfrew or Harry Rosen, because I'm usually tailed by over-attentive employees. If I'm paying cash at a restaurant, I will hand it to the server instead of leaving it on the table, to make sure no one accuses me of skipping out on the bill. If the cops approach, I immediately ask if I am being detained. Anyone who has ever travelled with me knows I experience serious anxiety when dealing with border officials—I'm terrified of anyone with a badge and a gun, since they always seem excessively interested in who I am and what I'm doing. My eyes follow every police car that passes me. It has become a matter of survival in a city where, despite all the talk of harmonious multi-culturalism, I continue to stand out.

I was carded for the first time in 2007. I was walking my bike on the sidewalk on Bathurst Street just south of Queen. I was only steps from my apartment when a police officer exited his car and approached me. "It's illegal to ride your bike on the sidewalk," he informed me. "I know, officer, that's why I'm walking it," I replied edgily. Then the cop asked me for ID. After sitting in front of the computer inside his car for a few minutes, the officer returned nonchalantly and said, "Okay, you're all set." I wanted to tell him off, but thought better of it and went home. I still don't know what he saw when he ran my name.

Over the next seven years, I was carded at least a dozen times. One summer evening in 2008, two friends and I were stopped while walking at night in a laneway just north of my apartment, only a few hundred metres from where I was carded the first time. Two officers approached in their cruiser, briefly turning on their siren to get our attention. Once they got out of the car, they asked us what we were doing. "We're just walking, bro," I said. The cops immediately asked all of us to produce identification. While one officer took our drivers' licences back to his car, the other got on his radio. I heard him say the word "supervisor," and my stomach turned. Within 60 seconds, a second cruiser, marked S2, arrived in the laneway, and the senior officer at the wheel got out to join his colleagues.

The officer who had radioed for backup returned and asked us to empty our pockets. As the supervisor watched, the radio officer approached us one at a time, took our change and wallets and inspected them. He was extremely calm, as if he was thoroughly accustomed to this routine. "I'm going to search each of you now to make sure you didn't miss anything," he explained. I knew it was my legal right to refuse, but I couldn't muster the courage to object. The search officer approached me first. "Before I search you, I want you to tell me if I'm going to find anything you shouldn't have," he said gravely. "I don't have anything," I replied, my legs trembling so violently I thought they'd give out from under me. The officer patted down my pockets, my pant legs, my jacket, my underarms. He then repeated the search with my two friends, asking each of them before touching them if he would find anything. One of my friends spoke up: "I have a weed pipe in my back pocket, but there's nothing in it." The officer took the pipe and walked with the supervisor to the car with the officer who had taken our ID. As the policemen huddled for what felt like an hour, my friend apologized. "It's not your fault," I replied. I cursed myself for choosing that route rather than staying on Queen Street, where hundreds of people would have been walking. Here, we had no witnesses.

When the officers finally came back, they returned the pipe to my friend. "Are any of you currently wanted on an outstanding warrant?" asked the search officer. We all said no. "Okay, guys, have a good night," he said. I was still too scared to move, and apparently my friends were too; we just stood there and looked at the cops for a second. "You can go," the officer assured us. I made sure not to look back for fear they'd interpret some outstanding guilt on my part. I was certain that the police had just documented my name along with the names of my friends, one of whom was carrying a pipe for smoking an illegal substance. This information would be permanently on my record.

Another time, as I smoked a cigarette outside a local community centre on Bloor West near Dufferin, a police officer sat parked in his car, glaring at me and scribbling notes. After five minutes of this, I walked over to his cruiser. "Is there a problem, officer?" I asked. The cop, a 30-something white guy, asked, "Oh, are you lost? You look like you're lost." His response was so ridiculous I almost laughed in exasperation, but instead I just repeated that I was fine. After a brief pause the officer rejoined, "Really? 'Cause you seemed lost." I had to remind myself that I wasn't going crazy. "I know why you're doing this," I told him before dashing my cigarette and going back inside. Whether it was motivated by ignorance, training, police culture or something else, the officer's behaviour sent a clear message: I didn't belong.

When I was a boy in Oshawa, my parents always greeted black strangers we passed on the street. As an adult, I have taken up this ritual in Toronto—it's an acknowledgement of a shared (if unwanted) experience. These days, when I meet other black people who want to talk about race, I feel comfort and reassurance. I was shopping at my local grocery store recently when an elderly white fellow tapped me on the arm and pointed to a black clerk shelving goods down the aisle. "You guys, you brothers," he said in broken English. It was one of those moments I was grateful for dark skin, to hide my embarrassment. "What do you mean?" I asked him. "You know, you and him, you guys brothers," the man repeated. "But aren't we brothers too, you and I?" I asked. He paused and smiled. "Oh, yes, yes!" As he left, the clerk and I exchanged a smile. It's nice to be around other people who know what you're going through.

After years of being stopped by police, I've started to internalize their scrutiny. I've doubted myself, wondered if I've actually done something to provoke them. Once you're accused enough times, you begin to assume your own guilt, to stand in for your oppressor. It's exhausting to have to justify your freedoms in a supposedly free society. I don't talk about race for attention or personal gain. I would much rather write about sports or theatre or music than carding and incarceration. But I talk about race to survive. If I diminish the role my skin colour plays in my life, and in the lives of all racialized people, I can't change anything.

Last winter, I asked the cops if I could look at my file. I was furious when they told me no: that the only way I could see that information was to file a Freedom of Information request. Each one can take months to process. One of my friends, a law student at Osgoode Hall, recently had his FOI request approved. When he finally saw his file, he learned that over the years cops had labelled him as "Jamaican," "Brown East African" and "Black North African." They said he was "unfriendly" with them, and that he believed he was being racially profiled.

I have no idea what I'll find in my file. Does it classify me as Black West African or Brown Caribbean? Are there notes about my attitude? Do any of the cops give a reason as to why they stopped me? All I can say for certain is that over the years, I've become known to police. That shorthand has always troubled me—too many black men are "known" through a foggy lens of suspicion we've done nothing to earn. Maybe if they really got to know us, they'd treat us differently.

Falling; Fallen
Krista Foss

THERE IS AN instant in every fall, between realization and impact, when foreboding slides into survival. *It will hurt, jeezus it's gonna hurt,* becomes in the same millisecond, *I will get up, deal with it, be okay.* The morning my bike brakes jammed while I was hurtling downhill on a busy city street, shame elbowed in between dread and stoicism. I flew over the handlebars and away from the unremarkable CCM dragged from a storage locker only months earlier. My daughter, just shy of two years old, was fastened into the bike's plastic child seat. She had on a cotton dress, jelly sandals the colour of raspberries and a helmet encasing her head in laminate, Styrofoam and Disney lions. Only seconds before, the air had tickled our throats with car exhaust and pollen and we were laughing.

The bike landed on the cement sidewalk with a thud followed by the scrape of its metal frame. I hit the asphalt face-and-elbows-first so my skin peeled like a scalded peach. The first thing I heard was my daughter's frightened, dazed whimpers. I scrambled over to her, unfastened her from the seat, removed her helmet and palpated her face, forehead and skull with gritty fingertips, searching—searching first for something terrible, then for reassurance. She was jarred, indignant, okay. The little stuffed dog she'd been holding had landed belly up in a prim civic bedding of coleus and begonias. A half-dozen good citizens came running. My elbows and chin were bleeding. My jaw was hours away from swelling mostly shut, making it hard to talk, almost impossible to eat for the next few days. Strangers leaned in to help us to our feet, to right my bike. Somebody retrieved the stuffed dog. I don't remember the face of the man who yelled at me, but I can still conjure the quality of his tone.

"Who do you think you are riding around with your child like that? What kind of mother are you?" he barked into the fine summer morning. I've had several worse falls. Truth is, I fall a lot. Yet that particular event, punctuated so baldly with a question about my character, my fitness as a mother, stays fresh. That one still matters, as if it were a reference fall, an axel from which the other stumbles stick out like spokes in the direction of their own meanings.

Another summer, just a few years before my pitch over the handlebars, I caught the edge of a sandal in a streetcar track while crossing a busy intersection on foot. There was the sensation of a popsicle stick snapping against my flesh before I fell forward, crawled to the curb and hailed a cab to the hospital. The resulting cast on my broken foot—it was lavender-coloured fibreglass and I swung it around like Captain Ahab's peg leg—started a flirty conversation at a bulk food store with the man who would father my daughter. So a fall led to an encounter, a falling in love and then out of it, and a falling toward something else, the hardest and very best part of my life.

I've come to understand that a good life, or any life, is a collection of stumbles—falling in love, in line, into habits or simply, apart; falling off the radar, off ledges, out of grace, out of favour, out of love, or just falling out—and that every fall, good or bad, is laced with an inchoate failure, a gush of death; even the pleasurable falls hold within them potential hurt and thus, transformation.

It's fair to say that falls have been the making of me.

The latter half of the 19th century was the great age of fallen women in literature, and as a bit of an expert in the downward climb, I find them irresistible: Emma Bovary, Anna Karenina, Edna Pontellier. Passion, pleasure, self-discovery were attached like soft-cheeked babies to the flimsy backseat of their bumpy rides with status, marriage, children and reputation. Yet the men of the 19th century who created these fallen women were invariably elevated by them. The obscenity trial for Gustave Flaubert's serialized version of *Madame Bovary* made the full book wildly popular when it was released in 1857. Émile Zola and Theodor Fontane would follow with their own tales of adultery, *Therese Raquin* and *Effi Briest* respectively. *Anna Karenina* cemented Leo Tolstoy's stature as a genius without peer in 1879. A year later, Guy de Maupassant was happily lionized for his first published short fiction, "Boule de Suif," the story of a prostitute whose actions reveal the hypocrisy of the upper and middle class passengers she joins for a stagecoach journey.

So when in 1899, the American writer Kate Chopin, who fashioned herself after Maupassant, unleashed her version of the fallen woman—*The Awakening*'s Edna Pontellier—she must have hoped for some critical torque, a bump in the late Victorian version of the Q-score.

Of course, it didn't turn out that way. Because Edna Pontellier isn't just another wife and socialite who risks everything for romantic love and sexual liberation; she's a woman who struggles with marriage and motherhood insofar as it encroaches on her essential self. She loves her children yet admits a simultaneous and unapologetic indifference to them: "She would sometimes gather them passionately to her heart; she would sometimes forget them." This must have been a discomfiting apostasy for a woman at the *fin de siècle*; I still feel unsettled by Edna's utter candour, her inability to fudge the truth to herself or others.

I grew up in the 1970s when the role of a mother was neither liberated nor overly scrutinized. It was not uncommon for my mom to send her kids—she had five of us in seven years—outside in the morning, shut the door with a relieved wave and wish us a good day. She never gelled with the mothers of our neighbourhood who were smokers, soap-opera fans and late-afternoon martini-drinkers but like them, she unfailingly had lunches packed in the morning, laundry pegged to clotheslines by midday and dinner on the table before dusk. And like the other kids, we enjoyed hours and hours of unmonitored freedom. By the time I became a single mother two decades later, parenthood was different: morphing into something less friendly and unremarked or, at its worst, a perverse blood sport of gifted testing, medicalizing frustration, alternative schooling, French immersion and raw food lunches, exotic summer internships, play dates, hovering, and heated debates over bed-sharing: in other words, an inexhaustible well from which to judge each other and ourselves. I felt suffocated, doomed to stumble.

Did Kate Chopin suffer any such neurosis about raising her six children? Certainly, she was acutely aware of her era's expectations of mothers. Yet her widowhood at age 32 was a kind of emancipation, according to one of her biographers, Emily Toth. Instead of chasing after a secure second marriage (and there were many men smitten with her), she fell in love with a married man, moved from Louisiana back to her mother's modest house in St. Louis, Missouri, read Darwin, questioned Catholicism, hosted salons with an erstwhile membership of anarchists, atheists and free love enthusiasts, and became a woman who as she wrote made "her own acquaintance." Importantly, she also began to write.

And in doing so she divined the singular torments of motherhood a century before I'd feel their bite. She expresses it through Edna Pontellier's wry observation of wealthy wives, "the mother-women" who populate the summer resort of Grand Isle, most ideally embodied in the form of the witty, charming and happily pregnant Adele Ratagniolle: "It was easy to know them fluttering about with extended, protecting wings when any harm, real or imaginary, threatened their precious brood. They were women who idolized their children, worshipped their husbands, and esteemed it a holy privilege to efface themselves as individuals and grow wings as ministering angels."

When I was thirty, alone with a new baby and carrying my one working lightbulb in the pocket of my bathrobe from room to room, I was effaced but wingless, suffering the self-conscious notion that I too had fallen, not only off the shiny pedestal of my own possibility but also the ideal of parenthood.

This seemed true when I found myself swiping rolls of toilet paper from café washrooms, shoving them into the baby bag. This seemed true when a cockroach teetered along the rim of my daughter's crib like some entomological circus act, moving so fast it risked dropping onto her flannel blankets, the curled fuzz of a plush toy, her soft, clean baby skin. This seemed true when for the next several weeks, I maintained a slightly manic campaign of bleaching everything, until eczema unzipped the webbing between my fingers with itch and ooze, and I had to wear winter gloves to bed. Perhaps it was most true on the balmy summer nights after my daughter had just begun to walk — our life circumscribed by the park and the green grocer, no car and no resources — when I began a compulsive roulette with shame, and left her sleeping alone as I bolted down the stairs of my three-storey walk-up apartment building to run around the block to the convenience store for a French mint chocolate bar and back again. And every night that I didn't get caught for abandoning my daughter, was another night I would vow not to risk it again.

Before the next night, when I would.

Was it an act of irresponsibility or reclaiming some small territory of the self a la the ever-escaping Emma Bovary? Even today, I waffle. I do know it was characterized by a singular fear—that somewhere in that two-block circuit, I would trip, smash my head into the asphalt, or fall under the wheels of a car and not get back to my child before she woke. And that risk, exciting and terrifying in the same moment, gave these escapes their piquancy of secrecy and shame, which itself presumed an imagined external arbiter, a critic, a better mother than myself.

Among the early critics of *The Awakening* were these better mothers—a few women writers who complained that so much good ink would be wasted on a portrait of such poor parenting. Yet this response can't be properly characterized without understanding Chopin herself. Toth describes her as unabashedly single, flirtatious and free-thinking. Her opinions and lifestyle made her enemies, male and female. This coloured the critics' take on her second novel which was described in reviews variously as "trite," "gilded dirt" the work of an "unholy imagination." Many of her contemporaries acknowledged Chopin's daring, her skill as a writer. Still these voices were neither powerful nor numinous enough to stop the free-fall of what had been a promising career.

In the 1980s when I was blowing whatever promise I felt I had as a failed engineering student slogging through an economics degree I wasn't interested in, I took an English literature course as an elective, and when it was over, the tutorial assistant personally thanked me for attending his sessions. It was the first and only time I have been thanked for being a student. And the TA sweetened his gratitude with a suggestion that I read Kate Chopin's *The Awakening*. It took me a long time to make good on his recommendation. But one day, the grateful TA— he had fine features and wore an Ecuadorean pancho—popped into my head and I finally went to the library and borrowed the book.

Similarly, as a struggling single parent to a young child I was abandoning nightly for French mint chocolate bars, I woke up one morning and remembered a bicycle mouldering in a storage locker. I felt the same sense of delight as if I'd discovered a forgotten $20 bill in my jeans pocket.

The bike itself was dull blue with thin stripes that gave it a ruby throat, a modest flash of ornament much like a northern bird. I bought a child's bicycle seat at the Canadian Tire for an amount so outside my budget it tightened my chest weirdly. The seat was bulky and wrapped in cellophane stamped with red ink warnings. I phoned up my father to see if I could borrow some tools and, as I had hoped, he came himself to attach the bicycle seat for me, reading aloud the weight restrictions and warning labels with a Scandinavian lilt.

If my father had any hesitation about aiding and abetting this form of transportation for his daughter and granddaughter, he kept it to himself. He was, after all, a man with some insight into how a fall can alter a life. By the time he was attaching the child's seat to my beat-up bike, he'd already been tripped up by two bouts of tuberculosis. There would be another. All three trials with the disease involved a fall of some kind: the first was geopolitical, the last two, simply slips on a driveway.

When he was 14 years old, living in small southern port of Norway, my father and his family were kicked out of their home by World War II's invading German soldiers. He was put to work as a stretcher bearer—carrying the bodies of injured and dying men in various stages of sepsis and gangrene, some literally dripping through the stretcher's canvas. He was a tall boy with corn-silk hair, glaucous eyes, and preternatural thinness who succumbed slowly to damp and poor nutrition and the privations of crowded quarters. TB was an inevitability. Near the end of the war, he was sent to a sanatorium to recover. When he was released, Norwegians were exorcising a national revulsion over being associated with Nazism.

There was also an ugly and largely un-discussed post-war rage against the some 50,000 women who had slept with Nazi soldiers (something Himmler not only encouraged but actively organized under his "lebensborn" program to increase racial purity.) Several thousand of these fallen women were interned in special camps, had their hair shorn or were expelled to Germany. Others were simply referred to as "German tarts" for the rest of their days. The spectrum of violation, boredom or desire that produced an estimated 12,000 children from these unions was never discussed.

According to newspaper reports of their subsequent struggle for compensation, the *tyskerbarna* or "bastards" were shuttled off to mental asylums and orphanages, subjected to abuse, ostracized and/or used as drug test subjects.

That this collective misogyny occurred in the same place that produced Henrik Ibsen, the creator of proto-feminist characters such as Nora Helmer, could be read as either consistent with or a contradiction of Norwegian character, depending on which of my relatives you ask. And yet within a few decades another Norwegian, Per Seyersted, the son of a women's rights activist born around the same time as my father, rediscovered and righted Kate Chopin's fallen reputation.

Seyersted was an unlikely literary redeemer: he'd spent 17 years logging and toiling in Scandinavian saw mills and pulp and paper factories before he landed in Boston to begin a career as an academic at the age of 35. By 1969, he'd penned a critical biography of Chopin and edited a two-volume set of her complete works, including previously unpublished short stories such as the daring, sexually charged, "The Storm." These two publications pushed Kate Chopin back out into the world for literary reconsideration, where feminist scholars gave her momentum and a place in the American literary canon.

My father meanwhile didn't get the post-secondary education for which he was so suited. But he read voraciously and peripatetically, filling the family bookshelves with spy thrillers, epic historical fiction, works of philosophy, biographies of important men and most impressionably, for me, a set of literary classics. If ours was a relationship fraught with sadness and a complicity of the unsaid, those bookshelves—what I borrowed from them and what I didn't—became their own kind of conversation between us. It was his copy of Flaubert's classic where I first encountered Emma Bovary when I was too young to appreciate the texture of her character, wanting only to acknowledge her romantic idealism and not her delinquent mothering or naive ambition. I gobbled up Emma's tragedy sitting in a dim basement family room with indoor/outdoor carpeting and furniture my parents had made themselves. Yet such reading allowed me to see my quiet, distant father in a new light, translate his consumptive thinness into a kind of romantic Euro-hipsterishness with his cigarettes, rakish cravats and an accent that shaved cool Scandinavian angles into English digraphs.

I don't remember the day the public health nurse drove up that same steep icy driveway where my father had fallen weeks earlier, knocked on our front door and asked questions that left my mother shaken. But that visit entered the family lore in the form of a menace that hemmed our comfortable freedom with imminent shame. In addition to the war memories he never talked about, he'd carried a crystalline tubercular mass from Norway to Canada, held like a smuggled secret against his ribs, a dormant, self-contained planet until the fall cracked it open. It fragmented inside his body, avoiding his lungs, but infecting his blood anew. This new form of the disease was a threat only to him so he was sick, but he was working. And because it could easily be misunderstood in our comfortable neighbourhood of split levels, septic tanks and children riding banana-seat bicycles, we didn't speak about it.

My father had surgery to remove the mass leaking disease into his body. It left a scar under his heart, in the shape of a sickle, a visceral purplish pink that puckered inward like a mouth. The cupboards lined up with quart-sized brown bottles filled with pills, which he took in handfuls, 48 antivirals and antibiotics every day. He went to his advertising job, and upon arriving home often fell onto the couch with fatigue. He lost out on promotions, was forgotten at many social events. Around him his five children fought over television programs, and second helpings of dessert, and as children always do, adjusted to his new presence, which was really a warm-blooded absence. Already a retiring sort—a man more accustomed to sitting in a teak recliner with a book and Manhattan than he was roughhousing with children—he slipped into a kind of stoic invisibility amidst our noise and crayons and dramas of territory and pecking order.

Decades later, in the basement of my apartment building where we put together the child seat on my bike, I felt a customary embarrassment around him. Here I was his middle child, the first of his offspring to get a university degree, but also the first to procreate and do so without a partner or prospects for serious work, without money or a car. My fall in his esteem perplexed him as much as me. It was hard to look each other in the eyes.

Still my Norwegian father got me back on my bike, by pulling it out of a storage locker, greasing the chain, checking the gears, attaching a 15-pound child's seat to the frame, and not questioning my reasons or my rights for wanting to travel this way.

Suddenly, my daughter and I could go further, faster. And what was available to us—cafés and different parks, the waterfront, the trails and friend's houses—burgeoned and became something else, a source of adventure, a trippy, raucous new freedom. The constrictions, the sacrifices and resentments of being a single mother fell away and so did my nighttime escapes. There were three flights of steps up to our apartment, and once I had mastered carrying the bike on one shoulder, and holding my daughter's hand in the other, we began to climb the steel stairs up the Niagara escarpment this way—400 steps in all. The bike took us into the woods to find waterfalls or to climb up a gorge. We both grew stronger and more fearless.

So there was nothing to say to the man who scolded me in front of a crowd, the day I fell face-first off my bike, and my daughter fell down with it. I picked up my child, hitched her on my hip, grabbed the bike with my free hand, and pushed past the on-lookers, the warm pressure of their Samaritan's palms and the wristwatches telling them they were late for work. I pushed past with a hot face and a swelling jaw and a sobbing child, and got down to the business of being ashamed away from their worried looks.

A bad fall, I was learning anew, can be a turning point, an awakening, or simply pissy, ill-humoured luck—humiliation, physical pain, a reminder that the universe is a smartalecky jokester with a cruel left hook. How we respond to a fall, each and every one, measures us against time, asks something from us, if only a bandage, a smarting splash of iodine, a shame-faced apology, a croaky love song, a not entirely forgettable book.

Edna Pontellier would fall from convention in order to awaken. But she did not come to the desperate, punishing ends of Emma Bovary and Anna Karenina. Instead, Edna's naked submission to the soft, warm gulf waters off Grand Isle, is a death apart, potent with the possibility of triumph. Or simply a miscalculation of strength. "They need not have thought that they could possess her, body and soul," is her final thought of her husband and children.

Kate Chopin would move forward too fast with her realist's frankness about sexuality and the personal sacrifices of motherhood and marriage, and her career would stumble as a result. Shortly after it was released, *The Awakening* was barred from some libraries. The planned publication of Chopin's next short story collection was cancelled. Seyersted's biography has her shunned by certain friends and important contacts. Five years later, it was if she had not existed, shut out by larger publishers, her novel fallen out of favour and out of circulation. She died from a cerebral hemorrhage after a hot August day spent at the St. Louis World Fair in 1904, a spectacle which included everything from the world's largest Ferris wheel, to gondolas floating through man-made canals, to a bear pit, according to Toth.

My father would fall again before my daughter was born, again on a wintry path, so that a remaining sac of TB, one the surgeons had not found, would again tear apart. But the drugs were fewer and better that time. And then several years later he would fall for the last time, in Quito, in the first days of a trip with my mother celebrating his 40th wedding anniversary. And this fall—compounded with the altitude, a troubled heart and the TB- weakened lungs—would be too much. What came home was a box of ashes, and another kind of absence, another thing we couldn't express in the tidy patterns of words.

After I left the place where we fell from a bike, there was a moment when I heeded the man's words: What was I doing? What kind of mother was I? I wondered if I was supposed to stop doing or being something, or start doing and being something else, and how far any of these things was from the person I actually was.

Later, when my daughter turned six, I got married for the first time, and for the first time, she had something that represented a typical, secure family: mom, dad, dog, house. Ten years into the marriage, after eating homemade pizza, splitting a bottle of wine and watching a rented movie with my husband, I walked upstairs became dizzy and blacked out. I fell sideways. My head hit the corner of a butcher-block counter, then landed on the white tile of the kitchen floor. When I came to, I remember how cool the tiles felt against my cheek, and how I wanted to stay there, because it was still, effortless. I could hear my husband rushing about half-whispering over and over: "Oh my God there's so much blood." (Head wounds are prolific bleeders. Even after it was cleaned up, the grout between those tiles remained vaguely umber.) I thought perhaps that I would die, or was dying, and I remember telling myself I should stay calm. I felt alone because every fall, no matter how many people congregate to help, is essentially a solitary act. Still, I felt okay. So that's what I told my husband. "I'm okay," I said from the floor. "You should probably call an ambulance."

We stayed up all night in the emergency room as my blood pressure inched back from dangerously low, to something like normal, and all the other tests came back inconclusive, and the doctor finally told us to go. We felt elated. We felt we'd come through something together, and for a while we were rescued from the low level of despair that had skulked our marriage. But that moment of aloneness on the cool tiles would haunt me, remind me of something unattended, the same way Edna Pontellier described her own outwardly content marriage as having a subtle and "indescribable oppression…like a shadow, like a mist passing across her soul's summer day." It wasn't long before the closeness fell away from us; we fell back into old habits, and so fell apart. Then my daughter had a mom, a dog, and a smaller, less desirable house. And I was like a fallen idol to her—this woman on whom she relied, who'd become the author of so much disruption and loss.

"What kind of mother are you?" the man had asked. It never occurred to me to say I was simply the kind who fell off her bike on occasion.

Within a week of that fall, my jaw was better. The brakes on my bike were fixed and my daughter and I had another two years of riding around together, her helmeted head bobbing against the small of my back, her trusting hands clinging to my hips, her cheeks brushed pink with fresh air and expectation. Because, whether it's a beginning or ending, a fall is only ever a hitch in momentum, an exhortation to get up and keep going and a reminder that something has to be risked for the imperative of movement or for joy—absence or injury, broken-heartedness, loss or criticism, even death.

Eventually, my daughter grew out of the child seat. A few months before my father died and just before I got married, I took her to the track of her elementary school and held the seat of her very first new bike, the one her grandfather had bought her, running behind as she pedaled. She kept looking back to check that I was keeping her steady, upright. "Are you holding on? Are you holding on?" At some point I let go, and she raced ahead of me for half the oval. Then she looked again, saw that I was no longer clinging to her, lost her balance, teetered and pitched elbows first into the limestone screening. There was a scrape that produced little berries of blood. There were tears. We went back to the track the very next day. She made it all the way around that time, over and over again. It was overcast. I watched her move away from me, her face lit with freedom.

In the Dying Hours of War:
the Fate of Two Brothers
Don Gillmor

IN MID-OCTOBER, 1918, my grandfather, Donald Mainland, was near Maurois, France, with the Fort Garry Horse. A welterweight— 150 pounds, five feet six inches, with sandy hair and grey eyes, Donald was older than some of the men in the trenches. His 25th birthday had just passed without notice.

Fifty kilometres away, Donald's twin brother Tommy was recovering from his second mustard gas attack. He had been overseas since September 1916, first with the 101st Battalion, then transferring to the 24th Victoria Rifles. In October, his unit was in France, heading toward the town of Aniche, north of Cambrai. Tommy was recuperating quickly from the second gas attack just as he had from the first, and he felt the guilty relief of the natural survivor.

He had been the first of the two boys to enlist, in December 1915. Donald followed in June, 1917. They were born in Sutherlandshire, in the north of Scotland, a part of the world with a long tradition of fighting—often among themselves if they couldn't find a suitable enemy. They'd come to Winnipeg as boys and integrated easily into a culture that had a heavy Scots influence. They were both fine athletes, playing baseball in the Winnipeg baseball league, and soccer for Fort Rouge. In the winter they played hockey. They worked for their father's construction company where Donald learned his trade of bricklayer.

Peter Mainland had been born in Shetland, and had inherited the largest farm on the island. A two-line entry in the local archives sums up his career as a farmer. "About this time the Grand Hotel was built in Lerwick and put in the first Billiard table to come to Shetland. Peter spent his time playing billiards and drinking whisky and after a time became bankrupt."

After this public ruin, Peter immigrated to Winnipeg where he started building houses. In 1907, when business was slow, he cut a few corners and was arrested for "Obtaining Goods Under False Pretences" and served three months in jail. When asked about the whereabouts of their father, the boys were told to say, "He went off to college." After the war started, business was slow once more. Goaded by their connection to Great Britain and by the lack of work in Winnipeg, the twins decided to enlist for overseas service. Perhaps they viewed it as redemptive, a way to get out of their father's dark shadow, but maybe they just wanted to put some distance between them.

War wasn't the romantic enterprise they had imagined, but in the autumn of 1918 they were optimistic; it could end any day.

Kaiser Wilhelm II had already been informed by the German Supreme Army Command there was no hope of victory, though neither of the Mainland boys could have known this. On Oct. 4, the German government had sent a note to American President Woodrow Wilson suggesting the possibility of an armistice. Even the hawkish General Erich Ludendorff declared the war had been lost (though he would later reverse this position). A peace was slowly building, though it came too late for thousands of soldiers on both sides, including one of the Mainland twins.

My grandfather spent his first few months of the war digging trenches near Main Street, in Winnipeg. He finally shipped out to England on the SS Grampion in February 1918, and by March he was in France. On March 23, Donald's unit took up a position between Le Four Croix and the Faillouel-Villequier-Aumont Road. It was my grandfather's first taste of trench warfare: rats, lice, disease and the percussive orchestra of shells, the shock every new recruit felt.

On August 10th during the battle of Amiens, the Garrys were advancing up the Roye Road, heading for Hill 100. The cavalry couldn't expand into the fields, which were blocked by trenches and barbed wire. So they galloped up the dusty road in a straight orderly line, perfect targets. All of C Squadron was cut down by machine-gun fire as they rode along the road. Within minutes horses and men littered the ground. The last rider died some 100 metres from the objective.

After that catastrophe, the Garrys weren't in action until October 9, when they advanced on Gattigny Wood, south of Cambrai. That was the same day the Canadian Corps captured the well-known city.

The Garrys, who were part of the Canadian Cavalry Bde. with General Henry Rawlinson's Fourth Army, were supporting the advance to the Selle River. Allied pressure had, by then, forced the enemy to withdraw to the Hermann Line which in that area—opposite the Third and Fourth armies—ran from Valenciennes south to the village of Le Cateau. While retreating, the Germans left a series of rearguards which provided lethal resistance.

On October 9 the plan was to move forward astride the old Roman road which ran from the village of Maretz to Bavay. Sixth Cavalry Bde. would attack along the right side of the road while the Canadian Cavalry Bde. would advance along the left side. Leading the Canadian attack, with four machine guns and a battery of the Royal Canadian Horse Artillery, was my grandfather's battalion.

Gattigny Wood, which sat directly in front of the Canadians, was still in enemy hands. The German machine guns on the right flank were the responsibility of one squadron of the Fort Garrys which steadily advanced and drove the enemy back. The left side of the wood was attacked by another squadron which charged and killed the Germans with their swords in close combat. Meanwhile, a charge over open ground by the Lord Strathcona's Horse protected the left flank of the Garry's attack and cleared out the enemy near the town of Clary.

Some 200 prisoners, a 5.9-inch howitzer and roughly 40 machine guns were captured. The commander of the British Cavalry Corps described it as "the best cavalry action carried out by any cavalry unit on any front during the war." Though by this late point in the war, what defined a successful cavalry attack was a relative term. This last bloody demonstration of 19th-century warfare came at a point when almost a million horses and hundreds of thousands of cavalrymen had been lost.

The Garrys were able to advance up the road and capture the village of Maurois, even before orders were relayed to capture it.

The Germans, however, still had a lot of fight left in them. There were desertions and doubt, but there were also pockets of fierce resistance.

On October 15—the day the Allied advance had forced the German Fourth Army back across the Lys River—my grandfather was scrambling for cover. He was hit by two bullets, one in his right thigh, and the other on the left side of his chest, near his heart. He lay on the field, bleeding, unable to move. Machine-gun fire continued above him. Around him, the crisp French autumn lingered, the perfect season. The end of the war was at hand—everyone said so. They would be home by winter.

Fifty kilometres away, his twin brother, Tommy, was moving toward Aniche with the Victoria Rifles. During his first month in the military, he forfeited a week's pay for being absent without leave. Two months later, he forfeited another two days' pay for the same offence. A wiry young man with a wild streak, he was restless for action. A lot of men were, until they finally saw it.

He arrived in France in September 1916. Ten months later, in a trench that bore no resemblance to the dry troughs he'd dug in Winnipeg, he heard the Strombos horn sound, warning of a gas attack. The Germans had become better at deploying mustard gas, waiting for the right winds. The heavy gas stayed close to the ground and poured into the trenches. The bugles and gas alarms only gave a few minutes warning, often less, and Tommy was able to get his mask on, but he still needed to be taken to the field hospital to recover from the poisonous chlorine. He noticed that the brass buttons of his uniform had turned green.

Tommy was gassed again in 1918, but recovered once more. While his brother was lying on the uneven ground not far from Inchy, Tommy was moving north and east, following the retreating Germans. He hadn't heard anything about Donald, despite their proximity. By November 8th, the 24th Bn. Was at the village of Dour, some 12 kilometres west of Mons, Belguim.

The fall weather was perfect and the men were awaiting orders. Peace, they had heard, would arrive within days. There was a mood of quiet celebration, and they organized a soccer game between the 24th and the 25th battalions. Those moments, playing in the late autumn sun, may have been the happiest of Tommy's three years in France. The exhilaration of a game he played well, the sense that home was close. Playing on that muddy field, surrounded by the recent destruction of war, France finally held a sense of promise rather than the death and ruin that he had witnessed.

But they were soon in action, moving east, pursuing a retreating enemy that was unsure what its role was. Some of the German infantry surrendered and there were mutinies in the ranks. But there was still intermittent shelling from the retreating Germans, who were unaware that their leaders, both military and political, had already conceded defeat among themselves.

On November 10, there was a church service at Petit Wasmes, a rare Protestant church, and Tommy attended. He had been raised as a Presbyterian though had drifted somewhat, but he sat in the stone church and prayed with the rest. They all prayed for the same thing—that they would wake up the next morning to peace.

They did, though it wasn't as simple as that. While Tommy was praying in the Petit Wasmes, the Allied Supreme Commander Marshal Ferdinand Foch and his chief of staff General Maxime Weygand were sitting in a small stone church at Rethondes, to the south, meditating on peace as the German negotiators looked over the terms.

The German negotiating team had arrived at the Forest of Compiègne on the morning of November 8, and consisted of Matthias Erzberger, a politician, Major-General Detlof von Winterfeldt and a few others. There was little room to negotiate. A sailor's revolt on October 29 in Kiel had spread across the city then the country. Kaiser Wilhelm II was on the verge of abdicating (and did so the following day, on November 9). And Germany's Chief of General Staff Paul von Hindenburg had stipulated that the Armistice be signed, even if better terms couldn't be negotiated.

At first it wasn't clear what the terms were. When the Germans took their seats at the large table in Foch's elegant private railway car, Foch asked Erzberger why he was there. Surprised, Erzberger replied that he was there to listen to the Allied proposals for peace. Foch said he had none. After some confusion, Foch said the Germans first had to ask for an armistice, then Foch would dictate the terms. Erzberger did ask for an armistice, and Weygand outlined the terms. Erzberger asked if they could declare a ceasefire while they were negotiating. He had to report back to the German government and it would take time and in those 72 hours thousands of lives would needlessly and certainly be lost. Foch wouldn't agree to a ceasefire and said the deadline for a German response was 11:00 am on the 11th.

At 2:05 am on Nov. 11, Erzberger said they were ready to sign. It took almost three hours to go through the terms. A few minor changes were made (the number of machine guns and aircraft the Germans were required to surrender was slightly reduced) and at 5:10 am he signed.

Ten minutes later news of the peace was broadcast from the radio station in the Eiffel Tower. Paris woke to a cold rainy day but the city quickly filled with joy, though many of its citizens stuck with the original deadline of 11:00 before it was official. There was that symmetry—the 11th hour of the 11th day of the 11th month. But at that moment, in the pre-dawn gloom of a French forest, the war was effectively over.

There was still that limbo though, those six hours. It was a destructive stretch, even by the horrific standards of the first modern war. On November 11, the American Expeditionary Forces on the Western Front suffered more than 3,500 casualties. The Canadians, British and French added thousands more. Altogether, there were almost 11,000 casualties on both sides, more than D-Day. The key difference was that the lives lost on D-Day were sacrificed to further the war effort. Those lost on Armistice Day were arguably the most futile in a war that would come to define futility as much as bravery.

After the war, a congressional subcommittee was formed to find out why there were so many American casualties on Armistice Day given that the military leaders knew peace was at hand. Why risk the lives of men to take ground they could simply stroll to in a few hours? There were accusations of careerism—that ambitious officers had sacrificed their men to pad their records. In the end, it came to General John Pershing, the leader of the American forces, to offer a dismal testimony that would be echoed a few decades later: he was following orders, in this case, those of Foch, who had instructed the Allies to pursue the retreating Germans with "a sword at their backs" until the final minute.

The morning of November 11th was rainy and cold in northern France, the sun obscured. The grey wasted fields blended with the sky. Tommy Mainland was in his trench. It was mid-morning and peace was upon them. Tommy climbed to the lip of the trench to scan the landscape. Perhaps he wanted a last glimpse of the battlefield. Three years of his life had been spent in battle. He had survived two gas attacks and countless close calls, had seen friends die beside him. Maybe he was thinking of home, the clean snow already covering Winnipeg. A sniper's bullet hit him in the chest, knocking him backward; a German sharpshooter who must have been lying in wait, scanning the horizon for his final target to present himself.

Tommy was taken to a field hospital where he was listed as "dangerously ill." By the time he got there, the news had arrived almost everywhere at the front: the war was over.

It wasn't of course. Colonel Thomas Gowenlock, an intelligence officer in the US 1st Division, wrote in his journal, "At last eleven o'clock came—but the firing continued. The men on both sides had decided to give each other all they had—their farewell to arms. It was a very natural impulse after the years of war, but unfortunately many fell after eleven o'clock that day."

Tommy lay in his bed for four days, pondering the irony of his years as a soldier, his recklessness, his charmed existence—only to end like this; gravely wounded after peace was declared though still not formally recognized. He died on November 15.

My grandfather survived his two wounds. He was first taken to a stationary hospital in Rouen, then transferred to Birmingham, England. He was discharged in January 1919 and came home alone. He had lost his twin, the closest thing to himself.

Donald understood the war to be a matter of luck and fate—a

bullet missing by centimetres, a sudden shift in winds that carries the mustard gas away, a machine gun jamming, an arbitrary moment chosen for peace to be declared.

Back home, Donald worked as a bricklayer, first in Detroit then in Winnipeg where he built the home that he and my grandmother lived in. He never spoke of the war. My father said that when he asked Donald about his experience in France, he would deflect the question with a joke. His wounds plagued him throughout his life. Eventually, he was unable to work.

Two months after I was born, he was watching the Edmonton Eskimos play the Montreal Alouettes in the Grey Cup. He was a westerner and when the west clinched the game—the result of last minute heroics from Jackie "Spaghetti Legs" Parker—my grandfather suffered an angina attack. He survived, though died of a heart attack five months later.

His experience of the war died with him. I have several photographs of him. In one he and my grandmother are standing beside a Model T Ford, in Detroit. He's wearing a three-piece suit and a hat. It was the 1920s and they have the optimism of that decade. Another photo shows him in the kitchen, with Donald comically raising a rolling pin as if to hit my grandmother, a caricature of domestic strife.

The most striking photograph was taken in Valentine's photography studio in London, England in 1917. He is standing in front of a mural that features a dappled grey sky. There is a small stone ruin beside him, two pillars still standing. Donald is wearing his greatcoat with his hands behind his back. The photograph is laminated onto a postcard; something to send home. It was a romantic evocation of a battlefield, designed to impart a sense of nobility and suggest that the subject had heroically survived. A backdrop created for those on their way to battle, not those returning from the horrific, too often meaningless slaughter.

War and Peace in a Robotic Future
Wayne A. Hunt

How do we govern our technology? The question has an urgent feel to it, not least because in international relations ours is now the era of drone warfare and unmanned surveillance systems—and this is only the start. At some point we can envision a future of robotic armies and autonomous systems of weaponry. Already, there is a wide range of non-military uses for drones: delivering pizzas is one use, surveying land and buildings from the air, another. This is just the start of a wider revolution in Artificial Intelligence, or AI, as it is called. Google has spearheaded the use of autonomous vehicles or driverless cars as a way to bring creative destruction to the automobile industry and to reduce the fatality rate on the highways. Robots are transforming the way we do war, in ways ranging from semi-autonomous machines that aid soldiers on the battlefield to incorporating high-tech capacities into combat gear.

But these are not the only applications: robots are changing the parameters of how we view human interactions with machines in times of peace. A state-of-the-art robotic hand, for example, has recently been wired directly into the brain of a man who suffered paralysis, thereby allowing him to "feel" his replacement. The hand was developed by the Applied Physics Laboratory at Johns

Hopkins University and was part of a research project funded by the US Department of Defense's Defense Advanced Research Projects Agency (DARPA).

DARPA is a fabled agency. Officially it forms a kind of think tank for the American military; it is the institution charged with bringing new technologies into the armed services; it recruits leading experts from other domains into highly secretive projects, and it does so with an annual budget of about three billion US dollars. The results speak for themselves. The Internet, GPS, and stealth fighters all originated with DARPA. It is the Google of the armed forces—the place where far-out or long-term or "moon shot" thinking is encouraged. There is a natural affinity, therefore, between DARPA and Silicon Valley.

But relations between California and Washington have not always been harmonious. The Secretary of Defense, Ash Carter, has made several high-profile trips to Silicon Valley to try to woo reluctant tech start-ups to work with the government on security issues. It has not been an easy sell—a government approach to anything does not go down well in a part of the world that glories in its defence of individual autonomy and libertarian rights.

This, however, is not the real reason why Washington has to come begging to the worthies of Silicon Valley. The big disruption (a favourite phrase in the Valley) came with the revelations of Edward Snowden. They showed the close relationship between a government with an insatiable appetite for hard data about people's private lives and the tech companies that were willing to share that data with government.

From Facebook to Google to Twitter to numerous smaller start-ups, targeted user data was of immense benefit to a number of tech companies that wanted to create whole new markets and scale up their activities. Concerns about personal privacy, to paraphrase Facebook's Mark Zuckerberg, were so, well, *yesterday*.

If the Snowden episode showed anything to the thought leaders of Silicon Valley, it showed that being too close to government would kick them where it really hurt, in their business model. Thus tech companies wanted, and continue to want, encryption that no one could crack.

But to say, as the leading thinkers of Silicon Valley said, that government should simply get out of the way and allow the leading geeks of their generation to think up new apps and new platforms for the latest iteration of disruptive technologies was to miss a vital point: Silicon Valley would be filled with groves of apricot trees rather than venture capitalists were it not or federal government support for research. The early corporate history of Oracle involved work for the Central Intelligence Agency while Intel worked with the Pentagon. Much of the rhetoric of leading Silicon Valley thinkers like Elon Musk and Peter Thiel is about a libertarian vision of the future (both were leading members of what was called "the PayPal Mafia" because of their connections with that tech firm), but the reality is that the working lives of these individuals have involved constant contact with government, either through e-commerce, Federal Communications Commission (FCC) decisions, patent law, corporate tax policies (as in politically charged questions about how much tax companies like Apple pay in the US), or with government counter-terrorism measures.

This last measure may preoccupy Washington decision makers, but it is safe to assume that the war on terrorism is not something that keeps the leading tech thinkers up at night. They have grander thoughts, the most powerful of which is about the direction that technology *itself* is headed—toward that point, often referred to as the "singularity," when machine thought replaces human thought. Developments in machine technology and in Artificial Intelligence (AI) *do* worry these people—and they have acted accordingly.

In the summer of 2015 the superstars of the tech and scientific communities sent an open letter to the International Joint Conference on Artificial Intelligence in Buenos Aires calling upon the governments of the world to ban the development of "offensive autonomous weapons." Signatories included the aforementioned Elon Musk and the cosmologist Stephen Hawking. Both had garnered over-hyped attention by musing, in public, about where AI would take the human race. ("The development of full artificial intelligence could spell the end of the human race," Hawking told the British Broadcasting Corporation, while Musk, in turn, called it "our biggest existential threat.") Signing on as well was Steve Jobs' cofounder of Apple, Steve Wozniak (the "Woz"), along with Skype co-founder Jaan Tallinn and Demis Hassabis, the chief executive of Google DeepMind—members all of the tech intelligentsia. Noam Chomsky added his name, as did numerous others.

The letter was clear about where all this was headed. It stated that:

The key question for humanity today is whether to start a global AI arms race or to prevent it from starting. If any major military power pushes ahead with AI weapon development, a global arms race is virtually inevitable, and the endpoint of this technological trajectory is obvious: autonomous weapons will become the Kalashnikovs of tomorrow.

Technology, in short, was seen to be getting out of hand. But it was important to remember the context. The letter was written in the face of two powerful and transformative technologies. The first had to do with climate change. There have been proposals to use technological fixes as a short-term remedy to the situation. Mechanisms like solar radiation management (as a way to reflect sunlight back up into the heavens) have been debated as a way to "hack the planet" in order to slow down the rate of climate change. These human attempts to redesign the global climate system are part of a wider package of geo-engineering measures that have excited public opinion around the globe. But the point is that although we have the technology to do this, we do not have broader political support for this. Ethics and politics are on a collision course. What, for example, would happen if nation-states changed weather patterns so as to bring on more rain? What would happen if non-state actors—such as wealthy individuals or, more controversially still, terrorist groups—started doing this? What international mechanisms could be put in place? And who would enforce these mechanisms?

But this is not all. The second great technological moment is coming with AI. Companies like Google see AI as the way of the future. In fact Google wants to evolve into a completely different entity, one that is future-oriented and based on a spectrum of new and emergent technologies—but with AI occupying a central place in this spectrum. (To reflect this thinking, a corporate restructuring at Google has recently taken place, with Google being one subsidiary—albeit the pre-eminent subsidiary—in a larger holding company that goes by the name Alphabet.)

To return to the letter about AI, it has to be pointed out that the same political vitriol that came out in discussions about geo-engineering is currently being redirected toward AI. The aforementioned missive from Hawking and Chomsky et al. worried that AI weapons systems are taking us down the proverbial slippery slope. They pointed out the parallels with the nuclear threat, going on to argue that:

Unlike nuclear weapons, they require no costly or hard-to-obtain raw materials, so they will become ubiquitous and cheap for all significant military powers to mass-produce. It will only be a matter of time until they appear on the black market and in the hands of terrorists, dictators wishing to better control their populace, warlords wishing to perpetrate ethnic cleansing, etc.

Continuing in this vein, the letter-signers noted that:

Autonomous weapons are ideal for tasks such as assassinations, destabilizing nations, subduing populations and selectively killing a particular ethnic group.

Hardly a happy prospect, that. But the scientists and academic experts listed in the AI-wary missive are on to something: the world does not need another high-tech weapon system. And sharing the world with nonhuman intelligence offers up a frightening scenario, but it should be pointed out how distant this prospect really is. They have an emotive force because these are arguments that have been shaped by fears raised in the movies and in the creative arts more generally.

Autonomous weaponry and robotic battles are, to take the easiest-to-hand example, the essence of science fiction. As such, they appeal to a small but fervent audience. When translated into movie making, however, the anxieties that are raised have a wider impact. And, again, ethical problems are raised. When does a part-human, part-robot act like a machine, and when does the same entity act like a human?

The question took on a cinematic urgency with the 2015 release of the British sci-fi thriller *Ex Machina*. As a movie, *Ex Machina* has some cumbersome moments, but it does soar when the visual chemistry of the actors comes together. The storyline revolves around a programmer named Caleb (Domhnall Gleeson) who is employed by the world's most popular search engine (guess who that is in real life?), called Bluebook. Caleb visits the high-security home of the company's CEO, a character named Nathan (Oscar Isaac). The only other person there is Kyoko (Sonoya Mizuno), a housemaid. Nathan has used AI to construct a seductive human-like robot called Ava (Alicia Vikander). Nathan wants Caleb to put Ava to the Turing Test, a mechanism designed to see if an AI entity can pass as human.

Psychological jousting ensues between Nathan and Caleb, but it is Ava who really twists the plot twists. Who can be trusted? In a key moment, Ava murmurs to Caleb (when Nathan is unable to hear), "You shouldn't trust anything he says." Ava is the unquestioned star of the movie, the *femme fatale* who puts on a dress, stockings, shoes, and a wig, only to remove them, in highly stylized silhouette, when she is certain that Caleb is watching. Paradoxically, it is half-human hybrid robots like this who manage to take method acting to a different psychological level, teasing out questions of mind-body relationships and equally deep questions of how we all come to terms with our own selves in an era of Machine Intelligence.

But it is not just art house movies that are concerned with robots. Robotic armies feature heavily in mainstream action movies as well. *Avengers: Age of Ultron* is a superhero movie released in 2015 and based on Marvel Comics characters. It plays to anxieties about AI as well. On this occasion the plot revolves around a machine creation called an "Ultron." The Ultron was created for peaceful purposes, but it has developed a god complex and does the exact opposite of what it was programmed to do. It believes that it must eradicate all of humanity in order to save Earth; an army of drone warriors are pressed into service to achieve this end. Other action movies have put variations on the same formula, with the recent *Star Wars: The Force Awakens* adopting a similar approach. Galactic battles between heroic humans and human-like machines, it seems, are a tried and true part of the Hollywood formula.

With so much emphasis on war, it is refreshing to find a thoughtful exploration of the other side of the equation, the use of robots in times of peace—a possibility that seems to be indicated by the brilliant and critically acclaimed television series *Mr. Robot*. Alas, *Mr. Robot* is not about robots. It is, at one level, about the many quirks of human existence in a wired world, but ultimately it is about advances in communications technology and how these advances make people robot-like. *Mr. Robot* stands as a metaphor.

With Christian Slater in the role of Mr. Robot, the protagonist is a mysterious anarchist. (Is he an Edward Snowden? Is this art imitating life, or the other way around?) Mr. Robot recruits a young security engineer named Elliot (Rami Malek) into a team of hacktivists. Elliot puts in a working day for a cybersecurity company and by night hacks the same company. Struggling with social anxiety disorder and depression, Elliot's thoughts are delusional. He uses morphine, but he does good by the world by foiling an online ring of child pornographers. (Real-world events form a distant but ever-present backdrop to events, thereby leaving open the question: Is it Elliot who is Edward Snowden? Or is it a blind alley to try to draw those comparisons?)

Billed as a techno-thriller, the series premiered on USA Network. It features constant plot twists and characters that have an aura of authenticity to them because, as with all great literature, just when someone expects a character to act in a certain way, they travel in a different trajectory, and Machine Intelligence, in its own way, amplifies these instincts.

Each of the episodes can be viewed as individual entertainment, just as the AI-centred movies serve as entertainment—but they also serve a deeper purpose. They allow people to think about the way technology has an impact both on their personal lives and on public institutions. When scientific advances in AI and in communications technology move faster than our moral understanding of where all this is headed, as they do now, people struggle to articulate their discontent. When issues like drone warfare and secret wiretaps and massive data mining enter the public domain, the traditional categories of right or left do not fit, and so too the traditional political remedies do not fit: expanding or shrinking the role of the state, which is the normal default position in politics, will not help the situation. But it does not end there. When issues raised by AI are placed on a more personal level, and society has to decide upon the moral quandaries of having machines look after us in our old age, the political language of right and left becomes stale, out of date.

Change is coming at a rate that outstrips the capacity of society to think about, and reflect upon, that change. Popular culture, in the form of cutting-edge movies and innovative new television programs, offers up a unique mental architecture. This same architecture gives people the space, and the time, to think about a range of scientific advances. And it allows them to do so in a way that makes sense to them. From this, we learn—or learn again—a fundamental truth: that those who work in the creative arts perform a vital, but often unrecognized, democratic service.

A Dozen Cups of the Dead
Michelle Kaeser

ONE BY ONE, I pick up the funerary urns. They're made of glass, of porcelain, of metal, of stone. There are dozens of them on display, and I don't know which to choose. I look at one made of wood. Dark wood, roughly the shade of Mom and Dad's kitchen cabinets. Is that a plus? Should the urn match the home décor? I test its weight, view it from different angles, try to take a look inside, make sure it would be pleasant enough in there for Dad. But there is no looking inside. The urn is screwed shut on the bottom.

"What's with these screws?" I ask the funeral director who's guiding this whole operation. She's a youngish woman, thirty-something, efficient and assured, just the slightest bit stern in her manner, ready for whatever variety of grief she might encounter.

"The screw-locks are a feature of all our wooden urns. They're very secure," she says.

No good. We want easy access to the ashes. Mom has plans to do a bit of scattering here and there. She's mentioned some sort of ceremony in the backyard, by the Happy Hour bench where Dad sat and drank his many after-work glasses of wine. And she wants to smuggle a few handfuls back to Switzerland, to return a fraction of him to the farm on which he grew up.

"Oh. But we wanted to scatter some of the ashes," I say to the funeral director.

She nods knowingly at this concern, we're an unoriginal family. "We can certainly have some of the remains set aside for you," she says. "You'll receive them separately, in a disposable container."

"Oh," I say, the word of choice in recent days. This whole process is stilted, filled with bumps and hesitations and meaningless *ohs*.

But firm decisions have to be made, many of them. The director holds a folder against her chest in which our every decision is neatly noted. And there are still too many blanks, there's no time for stumbling. She presses us along: "Is that what you'd like? Some of the remains set aside?"

"Oh. Okay. Yeah."

"And how much would you like us to set aside? Shall we say half a cup? A cup?"

Well now.

Half a cup? This is something new. This discussing my father in terms of measured cups. You can prepare for death, the logistics around it, the things that will need to be done, the people who will need to be called, and even to some degree the expected grief. But cups-of-your-father is a hard one to anticipate.

"I don't know how to answer that," I say. "How many cups are there?"

"Usually about twelve," she says in the same level tone, like she's giving me the recipe for a party-sized sheet cake.

"Well. Um," I say. Because what else do you say to that?

But the funeral director doesn't like this answer. She holds my gaze, urging more definitive commitments.

"Um," I try again. "Okay. I guess we'll take about a cup?"

She gives me a clipped nod and makes a note in the folder.

In his six-volume autobiographical novel, the Norwegian writer

Karl Ove Knausgaard writes about a distinction between our conception of death and death as it actually is. As a concept, death couldn't be more familiar. It exists in movies and books and songs and unending news reports. It's in our consciousness, it's out in the open, it's everywhere.

But as an observable reality, death is deliberately concealed. We quarantine it in hospitals and care homes, in funeral parlours and cemeteries. Actual death is too wild and unpredictable to be left out in the open. It has to be caged, like some zoo lion. And so it's pretty easy never to learn about death's most tangible features. That a body yields twelve cups of ashes, for example. Or that the ashes aren't ashes at all, but the fragments of crushed bone.

It wasn't always this way. It used to be that death was permitted, even welcomed, almost anywhere. The German philosopher Walter Benjamin, when writing about the disappearance of death from society, notes, "There used to be no house, hardly a room, in which someone had not died." Death happened all over the place. It happened in your home, right in front of you, right in your bed. And after it did, you'd just wash the sheets and carry on.

Now that sort of thing is creepy, even vulgar. As soon as we catch just a whiff of approaching death, we shunt the carrier away, to the hospital or hospice or whatever other place has been deemed appropriate for them to carry on with the unseemly business of dying.

I sit perched on the windowsill of Dad's hospital room. It's nicer by the window, the room feels more bearable, but only slightly. There's a strange quiet here that feels thick and uncomfortable.

"What do you want for dinner, Dad?" I ask, if only to break the silence.

He looks less like Dad these days, more like someone who's about to die. From some angles, I don't even recognize him anymore. His legs have shrunk, his head looks oddly round. I wonder at the change.

"I don't know," he says.

"We could bring you pasta. Or just a sandwich?"

"Ok."

He doesn't care. Not about this. He doesn't want to be here. He doesn't want to die here. But he will, of course. Because this is where we bring people to die. Always a place like this, institutional, impersonal, somewhere removed from the familiarities of their lives.

"You want some coffee? I could bring you a cappuccino or something," I say.

"I don't know."

"I'll bring you a coffee."

"That's fine," he says, almost reluctantly. Dad's not so chatty lately.

From another corner of the room, the quiet is interrupted by the sharp moans that emanate from one of the other two patients here, I'm not sure which one. They seem alike—the pall of death has begun to eclipse them both.

The trouble with the window perch is that it gives me a better view of these two. Here they are, lying within sight of me, just dying. Knausgaard writes, "We are constantly surrounded by objects and phenomena from the realm of death. Nonetheless, there are few things that arouse in us greater distaste than to see a human being caught up in it."

And that's just the word that comes to mind. Distaste. Veiling the sadness and the tragedy and the absolute ordinariness of their deaths is the distastefulness of it happening right in front of me. The sounds they make seem of a different range than the range I'm used to. These erratic groans and sighs and whimpers have a quality I don't quite recognize, the sounds of bodies struggling to shed themselves of life, maybe. I'm alert, like I'm in a place I'm not supposed to be, like I'm suddenly inside the zoo lion's cage and can hear its low growl in the corner. From nearby this growl seems to have taken on a whole new and much more terrifying tenor. Or maybe I'm just listening more carefully. Either way, I'm frightened.

But Dad doesn't seem afraid. What he seems is focused. He tries to stay very quiet when he can, like silence will protect him. But I wonder if he can sense, already, that in just a day or two he'll be reduced to cups of powdered bone. Twelve cups. Or maybe eleven. Dad's a small guy.

Benjamin writes, "Dying was once a public process in the life of the individual and a most exemplary one; think of the medieval pictures in which the deathbed has turned into a throne toward which the people press through the wide-open doors of the death house."

Deathbed as a throne? That's become almost impossible to imagine. There's certainly nothing regal about the rolling hospital cot. Maybe a cot is too generic, too obviously plebeian. Maybe it would be easier to imbue Dad's bed at home with a royal dignity. At least it has a headboard.

In the early days of Dad's final stay at the hospital, there's talk of this, of bringing him home to die. When it becomes clear that no more can be done for him, no further treatment will be administered, we float the idea of settling him at home for the duration.

But for one reason or another that doesn't happen.

Of course there's always one reason or another why that sort of thing doesn't happen anymore. Almost everyone dies in a hospital now. Statistics have it that about eighty percent of Canadian deaths happen in hospitals or hospices. This despite over eighty percent of Canadians expressing a definite preference for dying at home.

Dad's no exception. He wants to come home. He asks to come home.

"Can we do that? Can we bring him home?" we whisper to each other, hoping Dad won't hear.

"Maybe we can do that?"

"Let's think about it."

We go through all the motions of considering this request, and then we go through the further motions of raising various logistical, very practical, objections to it. But the real reason we don't bring him home, of course, is the almost cultural sense that death is best kept in its place.

"So this is our casket room," the funeral director tells me. This is a year after Dad's death. I've come back to meet with her, because I'm interested in people like her, in these intermediaries who stand between us and the particularities of death. And I'm interested in trespassing on the spaces of death—I'm worried that I've been missing out on too much by keeping my culturally prescribed distance.

The first thing the funeral director shows me is the wall of caskets, the different colours, different woods, different price ranges.

"Which one is most popular?" I ask.

"It really depends. But something I've seen a lot lately is families going with the simple pine casket." She points to the cheapest offering in the room, a plain wooden box. "Then the families bring markers or sharpies to the service and have the visitors actually sign the casket."

"Huh."

What exactly do people sign on a casket? *Thanks for the laughs! Say hi to the Big Man for me!* Do they write lame jokes? Or even clever ones? At least some mourners must feel puzzled over what to write. I imagine them left standing before the casket holding bright magic markers and struggling to find something sufficiently solemn to doodle.

"Neat idea," I say.

"Isn't it? It personalizes the services."

But I wonder about the implications of replacing the more traditional rituals of mourning with an exercise like this, one that's more palatable, more familiar, more pleasing and comfortable. Something must get lost when you replace the solemn, reflective regard for death with the nostalgic fun of signing a cast or a yearbook. There seems to be some avoidance at work here, as though this is just another way of pushing death away, of evading any real thoughts of it or contact with it, a further repression of our fears.

As the funeral director continues the tour of the facilities, describing one feature or another, I notice that avoidance is pretty common. Euphemisms abound. She talks of *the loved one*, not the corpse, not even the deceased. She talks of *services*, never funerals. She points out *event spaces* and *gathering areas* and *arrangement rooms*. This whole venue is referred to as a *visitation centre*, not a funeral home. Even here, in this house of the dead, death somehow feels far away.

In the planning of Dad's funeral, Mom decides I should give a eulogy. She offers no words of advice, except these: "Make it personal. I want it to be very personal."

"Of course," I say. I can't think of any other way to approach it. "What else would it be?"

"The whole funeral needs to be very personal."

"Of course," I repeat.

And we're right on trend with this longing for personalization. The funeral director marks this as one of the most notable shifts in practice in recent years. "People are looking for ways to make their services unique. It can be in big ways or small ways, but the trend is for more individuality. I'd say that's one of the biggest trends we're seeing," she says.

This is hardly surprising. After all, we live in a time in which everything is personalized, individualized, customized. Our understanding of the self is starkly individual—an effect of the Me Generation, maybe. Or maybe its cause. We seem to pay relentless attention to identifying tiny differences that exist among us. We search for these slivers of distinction and then inflate them out of all sense of proportion. In this way, everyone gets to be spectacularly special. Everyone wondrously unique. We are a generation of extraordinary people.

As I compose the eulogy, I think of the ways in which Dad was most extraordinary. I draw only at the anecdotes that showcase his oddities, the things that make him uniquely Dad. No point in including any generic moments of paternal love. Those seem somehow trite in the telling.

"How's it coming along?" my brother asks me. We're sprawled out in the living room, notepads in hand.

"Okay, I guess. You?"

Mom has tasked him with writing a eulogy, too. It doubles the chances of a truly personal tribute.

"I don't know. Not great. I need some better stories here," he says.

So we trade memories, we compare funny stories about Dad, we compete to see who can recall the most distinctive of them.

There's something comforting about this process of searching for the things that set Dad apart from everyone else. It lets us cling to the idea of him as an individual, alive and clearly defined. But it makes the task become one almost entirely removed of any real acknowledgement of death. Instead, it's all about life.

Fear of death is an occupational hazard for humans. The loss of the self, the annihilation of our individuality…it's all very terrifying. But Ernest Becker, in his Pulitzer Prize-winning book *The Denial of Death*, identifies another fear that is just as pervasive: the fear of life. This is a fear of separation, of individuation. Being alive means standing apart from the cosmos. It means existing as a distinct, unique creature. The very things that mark us as alive— the boundaries of our bodies and personalities—they also separate us from the rest of the world. These demarcations can make us lonely. And boy, that, too, can be terrifying. Apparently we're about equally afraid of both, and we spend our days bouncing around between these twin terrors.

Becker explains, "On the one hand the creature is impelled by a powerful desire to identify himself with cosmic forces, to merge himself with the rest of nature. On the other hand, he wants to be unique, to stand out as something different and apart.…You can see that man wants the impossible: he wants to lose his isolation and keep it at the same time."

What a ridiculous species we are! It's nothing but one paradox after another. We want to merge with the cosmos and we want to stand out from it. We want union and we want individuation. We want death and we want life. Our fear of the one threatens our desire for the other, so we're forever balancing the scales.

But what happens, say, when a culture becomes fiercely individualistic? When personal considerations trump any collective ones? When the importance of standing out becomes paramount? When it's no good to be ordinary anymore, when it's a failing to just sort of blend in with the crowd, with the cosmos?

Well, what happens is the scales tip.

It's no accident that the cult of individuality has coincided with the quarantining of death. The less room we make for death—the less we're forced to think in terms of a collective enterprise, the more room there is for flourishing individualism. These things exist in tandem.

At Dad's wake, I receive condolences and sympathetic smiles and kindly-offered characterizations of the man he was. These all take on a similar theme.

"Your dad was one of a kind."

"He was a piece of work."

"A real original."

One woman clasps my hands between her own and gives me this advice: "Just remember what made him special. Always remember that." Like it's dangerous to remember instead what made him common.

We seem to have become so busy fending off anything that encroaches on our sense of individuality that we've forgotten to worry about threats to our sense of union, of community, of sameness, of subsumption. We've forgotten to guard against the horror of isolation. We're a culture with a loneliness problem.

The moment Dad dies, there's no family with him. Just a nurse. We're at home trying to get some sleep when the hospital calls to tell us things look grim.

"Let's go, let's go, we have to go," Mom hollers to my brother and me, hoping we'll make it in time.

But we don't. We arrive to find Dad, or what used to be Dad, some version of Dad, perfectly still on his hospital bed, his death throne.

"It's not right," Mom says as she weeps. She feels guilty about having let him die alone, she feels negligent. "I should've been here."

I feel the same way. Part of me does, at least. The part that wanted to watch it happen, the moment, the actual release. The idea of it terrifies me, of course, but I'm drawn to look nonetheless, in the same way I'm drawn to look at any of the things that frighten me. The way we peek through our hands to watch a scary movie.

Presumably there wouldn't have been much to see in the exact moment of his death. He would have been breathing, and then he wouldn't have been. That shouldn't be so scary. It seems ordinary enough. Too ordinary, maybe. We don't like ordinary. There's a terror in the great banality of death.

Knausgaard ends the first volume of his opus with a study of such banality. He writes, "Death, which I have always regarded as the greatest dimension of life, dark, compelling, was no more than a pipe that springs a leak, a branch that cracks in the wind, a jacket that slips off a clothes hanger and falls to the floor."

The nurse who's with Dad when he dies describes the passing with little more excitement than one of these Knausgaard metaphors. There's nothing particularly interesting about the way Dad dies. Nothing that makes it special. He just dies. And that's that.

We receive Dad's ashes as promised. There's the urn that holds most of him and then the cup of him that's been set aside in a disposable container, a heavy-duty plastic bag, zip-tied.

In the backyard, we cut away the zip tie and open the bag to get at the ashes.

"Don't touch that stuff with your hands, eh?" my brother says.

"Why not?"

"I don't know. It's sort of…uncouth, isn't it?"

I grab a pinch of the ashes. What I'm touching doesn't even look like ashes. It looks like some finely ground spice. Something like cardamom, but a little duller in colour. I rub the ashes between my fingertips then flick my brother with these bits of our dead dad.

"Don't fuck around," he says.

"Why not?" I ask.

We take turns pouring fractions of Dad onto the grass by the Happy Hour bench. Mom spills some ashes, then I do, then my brother does. But a whole cup of ashes is rather a lot, as it turns out. Far too much for a simple symbolic scattering. We make it through about a quarter cup before the ceremony seems redundant. Banal.

So we seal the heavy-duty plastic bag—with a twist-tie this time—and we head back inside, where we linger around each other by the kitchen table, for just a little bit longer. I'm not sure why we do this. Maybe it's for the sense of community that arises when there's been a death, a togetherness that comes not just from the physical gathering, but from everyone understanding that this is the trajectory. We're all on our way to becoming pinches of something that looks like ground cardamom, sprinkled against bright green grass. Or maybe there's another reason. We've been forced into a confrontation with death, however tepid and restrained that confrontation has turned out to be. We've been forced into the places where death is still permitted to exist. Death feels closer than usual now, and maybe there's something primitive in us that longs to keep it near.

This doesn't last long. Soon we disperse, away from the kitchen table and away from each other. We carry on with our lives, focusing on ourselves, our own problems, our own goals, resuming the strict narcissism demanded by our culture, and we try to think very little of death, stuffing it instead back into the shadows.

Mom takes the plastic bag of ashes and puts it somewhere out of sight. I haven't seen it since. The urn, an unassuming wood box, dark wood to match the colour of the kitchen cabinets, gets set on top of a dresser. It looks like it could be anything, any one of those common household knickknacks that get assembled over the years, maybe a jewellery box, or a souvenir from some far-off country. It just sits there, quietly present, but relegated to its place, drawing no particular thought or attention. I'm not sure anybody really looks at it anymore. I'm not sure anyone has touched it since.

Playing God
Richard Kelly Kemick

I CAN'T REMEMBER not wanting a miniature Christmas village. It's like how I can't remember when I first realized I have bad posture: some things you never have to learn about yourself but rather just have to accept.

I moved out of my parents' house at seventeen, but my heart has never left—not out of some romantic notion of remembering my roots, but because the idea of renting an apartment with enough room to store my Christmas village borders on lunacy.

So now I am back in Calgary, hauling an unending line of boxes out from my parents' basement and into their dining room. My mother has already resigned herself to hosting next week's dinner party for twelve around the kitchen counter.

Once all the boxes have emerged from their summer hibernation, I begin.

I move west to east, starting with my six houses, the bourgeois ones placed closer to my church. Then there is my public park, which includes a hockey rink and two-dozen towering conifers. If you're lucky, you'll spot the deer. To make your way downtown, you'll have to traverse the Kemick Canal, its crinolined torrents now fully frozen. To cross, you have two choices: the Voltaire Viaduct, stony and austere; or the Pont de la Paix, wooden and ornate and fragile.

Once you're downtown, the streetlights will guide you. First comes my gift shop and then my bank, both of which boast extended weekend hours. Sovereignty Street is bustling with shoppers. On the corner is a string trio busking. Then there's my theatre, my hotel, my millinery. When I unpack my restaurant, I am awash with nostalgia. It was my first piece; I was in grade nine, and it was a gift from my mother. My parents were hesitant to buy it for me, thinking I didn't understand what I was asking for. But I knew exactly what I was getting myself into.

Look at me now, at twenty-five. Gaze on the world I've created. Just past my restaurant is my butcher. Next is my fire hall, my school, and my post office: public monies at work. At the far end of the village is my department store. And sitting in its display window—brace yourself—is a miniature miniature Christmas village.

Rising behind the department store is a modest hill. Rising behind that is a full moon, upheld by an adjustable stand. The moon is the first piece I bought for myself; I wanted to give my village a certain gravitas, and it did just that. It is, by far, my most commented-on piece. In fact, I am so intoxicated with it, I hardly notice that when it turns on, it emits a faint but constant squeal.

Once the buildings are in place and the villagers are snug in their beds, I link my eighteen adapters into one long chain of industrial power strips. Then, aiming the metal prongs of the master plug at the socket, I take a deep breath and look at my dark city. It is so close to being alive. And I am filled so full with wanting; it is all I know.

My wife, Litia, and I live in Vancouver. From our apartment, it is a forty-five-minute bus ride to Christmas Traditions, the nearest pop-up holiday shop. As I ride the bus, I mentally scroll through the Rolodex of things Litia and I can cut in order to bank even more of our paycheque. Here, of course, I use the word *our* in its most liberal sense, since Litia is the only one who receives a salary.

I like to think of our one-bedroom, 396-square-foot basement apartment as a museum exhibit on the lengths my generation has to go in order to stay debt free. I've rescued all of our plates from alleyways; our cutlery comes from the spillover sections of Salvation Army drop boxes. And I try not to make eye contact with our dog, Maisy, while I sneak dried rice into her kibble.

My wife doesn't realize that I've been selling articles of her clothing for the past three years. We've been living together for only two. "Where'd that striped top go? " she asked once. I feigned ignorance and then inconspicuously checked our Kijiji account to make sure I'd deleted the ad. I got a whole $23 dollars for it.

By the time I get to my bus stop, I've settled on cutting out grapefruit, coffee cream, and Halloween candy. We can also disconnect the land line; I'll use Litia's cellphone to make my fortnightly call home to Calgary. If we're being robbed while Litia's at work, I won't be able to call 911, but then, we don't have anything to steal.

At the strip mall, the Christmas store is near a Mongolian grill and a now-defunct Magicuts. I arrive twenty minutes before it opens, which gives me time to pace the windows and vow to not spend more than $20—plus tax, of course.

I've often wondered how my parents really feel about my village, the ceramic sprawl that's been growing with the force of manifest destiny and that now occupies the entire dining room table. I think my mother likes the village, not only because the woman is insufferably supportive of everything I do, but also because I'm fairly confident she takes credit for it when I'm not around. "Oh, this?" she tells her friends, gliding her hand over the houses despite my strict no-touching policy. "This is just a little something I've been working on over the years."

But I'm less sure about my father. I find it difficult to believe that the man who implored me to reuse duct tape and not to throw out asparagus elastics can look at my village and think anything other than, *Doesn't he still owe me $4,000 for the car?*

Still, he cannot be blind to the positives. Unlike my brother, who misspent his youth, I frugally saved mine. While Tress was out burning tire treads in the Presbyterian church parking lot, I was at home, polishing my miniature bird bath. While he was out having unprotected sex with his on-again, off-again girlfriend, I was crazy-gluing wreaths onto micro-lampposts. And the very night he ran a red and T-boned a minivan, I was in the dining room, dusting my cityscape with fake snow.

My village was also the impetus for the only time my father accompanied me Boxing Day shopping. How else could he ensure I not spend more than the minimum on things with, as he put it, "absolutely no resale value"? When the sliding doors at Canadian Tire opened, we quickly became separated in the churning crowd. I wound up blocked in by shoppers on the far side of the Christmas clear-out section, completely opposite the village display. The two tallest people in the store, my father and I, were able to make eye contact as he stood right where I wanted to be. Over the heads of shoppers, I hollered, "Get the chocolatier." But my father is completely deaf in one ear and 75 percent deaf in the other, and confusion darkened his face. In response, I scrambled up onto the side of a shelf and cupped my free hand around my mouth: "Get the motherfucking chocolatier!"

The night Litia found out about the village was the night she first met my family. My parents were in Vancouver for my brother's birthday, and we all met downtown for dinner. Litia and I had been going out for only a month, but we'd been sleeping together for three.

Upon introduction, my mother—seeing her greatest chance at grandchildren miraculously appear before her eyes—began to talk, and never stopped.

"I'm sure you must love to read," she told Litia. "Richard loves to read. When he was small, we would always go to the library. But he only ever wanted teeny little books."

"Pardon me?" Litia said.

"We'd wander the aisles," my mother continued, "and I'd ask him if this one or that one was small enough and he'd scream, 'No, they need to be *teeny* little books!'"

As my father, brother, and even the waiter laughed, I sat there, debating whether or not it would be possible to slit my wrists with the teeny little cheese knife. But my mother was not done.

"It must be why he loves that village," she said.

"What village?" Litia asked.

Like I said, it had been just one month since I'd stopped getting the milk for free, and I was still unsure whether Litia was "village material."

"Oh, Richard has a Christmas village," my mother said, and began to explain it in painstaking detail. And while I listened to her confuse my post office and library, gloss over my recreation area, and completely fuck up my all-embracing vision, I became assured that there was only a teeny little chance that Litia and I would ever have sex again.

I've stopped telling people about my village. Not because I'm ashamed of it. All I have to show for my quarter-century on the planet are two worthless arts degrees, my job as a self-employed dog walker, and a book of poetry destined to sell fewer than twelve copies. My Christmas village—bustling with eighteen buildings, more than sixty people, and countless accessories—is probably the most impressive thing I'll do with my life. And I'm okay with that.

What cash-strapped young man can look himself in the mirror and proclaim, Today I am finally going to buy that $22 miniature hedge with the two raccoons poking out? How do I explain to my mother-in-law, when she asks how the writing's going, that I wrote only 120 words today while her daughter was teaching grade six French, because I'd spent the afternoon cruising an Internet thread about mini-trees? Why, at 2:30 am, when Litia stumbles out of bed to the bathroom, do I find myself slamming my laptop closed, leading her to assume I had been watching porn rather than a speculative video on whether master creator Cynthia Shalev would release a synagogue that shines and shimmers with LED lights?

Of the few people I have told, each has a different theory. My mother—she of the goddamn "teeny books" story—thinks it is a fascination with scale. My cousin Alice, ordained with a human resource–management degree, informed me once that it is the ritual of collection that draws me back. My friend Alex and his boyfriend, Garry, both think it's because I'm gay. Each argument has its merits: scale is fascinating; I obviously enjoy amassing these things; and Maisy has often heard me wonder aloud why there's no such thing as Olympic synchronized swimming for men.

But none of those theories captures the visceral force that propels me.

A few years ago, before I met Litia, I was in a store at a Christmas shopping extravaganza in Edmonton. It was deserted when I heard the sleigh bells jingle above the front door. I turned to see a young woman, copper coils of hair bouncing off her shoulders.

I was struck into stillness as she walked straight to the villages. I watched her peruse the accessories section, gliding her delicate hand across the treetops, finally coming to rest on a small bundle of firewood. Seeing my in, I complimented her on the piece. "The reality of heating," I told her, "is often overlooked."

"Do you have a village?" she asked.

"Yes, I do," I said. "It boasts a population of nearly 200." Sure, I was lying—but who doesn't fib about size?

"Mine's much more modest," she said, blushing slightly. "But I recently found a three-storey brick apartment building with a café beneath."

"It's so rare to find porcelain brick," I said.

"And I found a pub with a straw roof," she added.

"That's beautiful," I said. "I hope someone doesn't blow it down." And we laughed together, breathlessly. "Tell me," I said, "what does your skyline look like?"

"I bought some mountains last year," she replied, "as a backdrop. They're cragged and plunging."

"Mine has a moon," I said. "It's full and white and throbs with song."

It is the closest I've come to having sex without ever touching the other person.

"Why do you collect?" I asked, desperate for clarity, hoping that her answer would reveal my own. "What drives us to this?"

She ran her fingers through her hair. "I'm expanding my mother's collection. She died of lung cancer a couple years ago." She paused, then opened her eyes wide to dry them.

"What's your story?"

If only I could've been lucky enough to have lost a loved one to a horrible disease and then channelled that inconsolable grief into miniature streets of snow-tipped cedars.

"Oh, you know," I said. "Pretty much the same."

The twenty minutes finally pass and Christmas Traditions opens up. Every holiday store is laid out the same. You're greeted by a sign that proclaims how many days are left until December 25. Today it's seventy-three. There's a clerk who greets you, usually an octogenarian. She asks if you need help, but if you're like me, you know where you're going.

At the front of the store, there are the tree ornaments. Past the ornaments is the tree lighting, and past that is the nativity section. Why anyone would ever need a pocket-size Baby Jesus just to remember whose birthday party this is, is beyond me. (If, however, it's a *miniature* pocket-size Baby Jesus, set within a village square nativity, then show me to the checkout.)

The villages are always set up at the very back, the hundreds of porcelain faces all frozen with Christmas love. And here, bathed in the dim lighting and cocooned in the airtight silence, the display holds the forbidden grace of a tabernacle.

An elderly woman walks up beside me. Her snow-white hair is freshly permed. Two gold chains hang around her neck. She is eyeing the gin distillery. I can tell she's unfamiliar with the piece because she raises an eyebrow when the water mill actually rotates. As I pretend to appraise a picnic table's paint job, I watch her; I want to see her reaction to the distillery's three-figure price tag. I've yearned for that piece for years, my porcelain white whale. But I can't get a distillery until I get a police station, and I can't get a police station until I get a city hall. Instead, there's a Batman tree ornament atop the church spire. For now, vigilante justice is the only justice my village needs. I fear a distillery will upset this delicate balance.

On this October morning, Christmas songs crackle through the speakers. At the front of the store, the cashier is grinding her chin into her chest, hopefully just sleeping.

The more the woman looks at the distillery, the more in love with it she falls. The stone and mortar smokestack. The light bulb inside that flickers like fire. Her hands shake slightly as she places it into her basket. She never even checked the price.

Back on the bus, I lovingly place the $29 juniper tree onto the seat beside me. And I say a small prayer for the elderly woman; I ask that the distillery turn her village into Sodom and Gomorrah and that her smiling citizens, hopped up on liquor and lust, eat one another.

There are three unshakable tenets that inform the creation of any proper Christmas village: scale, functionality, and style. The first is easily upheld by not switching between manufacturers all willy-nilly; having an elephantine flower vendor sitting beside a cart half her size will make it seem as if the vendor has an inoperable thyroid condition. Choosing a size is like driving in Toronto: once you pick a lane, you're in it for life.

Functionality, by contrast, requires a more seasoned eye. "What kind of town has this many fucking pharmacies?" I once asked my friend's mother, who had recently begun her own collection. "A town populated by meth addicts, Sharon. That's what you've built here." (Truth be told, you could get away with the three pharmacies Sharon had—especially as one of hers was clearly labelled an apothecary. I was just hoping that she'd be humiliated and offer me one.)

The final tenet, and by far the most important, is style. There are many different styles to choose from. Classic brands include Disney, Rudolph, and A Christmas Carol. They're referred to as sets because, like Happy Meal toys, there is a finite number of pieces you can acquire. Each year, Disney creates a few new ones, while the companies that make Rudolph and A Christmas Carol annually release a small number of scenes from the holiday films for which they're named: Rudolph learning to fly, Bob Cratchit carrying his son. Last year, there was a piece depicting the Bastille-like liberation of the Island of Misfit Toys, and one of Scrooge bowing to public pressure and squandering his life's savings.

For those who collect the sets, the appeal is that there is an end in sight. After your initial buy-in, you need only a couple of new pieces each year for your village to be the best it can be. Sets are the equivalent of the kid's table—somewhere safe to sit, where everything is served to you.

In the land of Christmas villages, what separates the kids from the grown-ups is moving out from the structure of the set and into the chaos of the classic. Classic villages are bound not by theme but by era—Victorian, 1950s America, modern— all produced by a variety of manufacturers. Such villages have no structure and can sprawl forever. They're where the big boys go to play.

The 1950s era revolves around boxcar diners, Coca-Cola, and an obsession with painting everything checkered orange. There is also a terrifying prevalence of motorcycles, whose riders are all helmetless. (I've yet to find the piece depicting the stacks upon stacks of human bodies that such a village's icy roads must claim each year.)

The modern era is loosely modelled on the skyline of New York but also features monuments from around the world, giving it a tawdry Las Vegas feel.

I've chosen the Victorian era for three reasons: First, it's the classiest. Second, since I'm not a James Dean enthusiast, McCarthy sympathizer, or closet racist, I have no interest in the 1950s. And third, if I were satisfied with living in the modern era, I wouldn't need a miniature Christmas village in the first place.

The Victorian era boasts taverns with names such as the Smoking Bishop and the Dirty Owl. There's even an ornament shop called Lily Bros. Gazing Balls. But there are two downsides to collecting this era. The first is that, just as real-life Victorians had to struggle to pay extortionate rents, I too have to wrestle with unfettered inflation. A top end Victorian building will run you between $100 and $200, while a person comes in between $20 and $50. The second downside is that, just as real-life Victorians had to heat their homes with coal mined by children, I too have to live with the unsettling necessity of child labour. This is not unique to the Victorian village but is spread across all eras, as ubiquitous as Christmas. Sometimes on Christmas Eve, I lie awake and think of sooty hands toiling in Sichuan factories, fingers delicate as tinsel, the paintbrushes like magic wands, touching life into blank human faces.

Litia and I used to travel quite a bit for school. Now we travel quite a bit for her work. And something I've noticed—whether we're in Vancouver, Toronto, or Montreal—is that a city is made alive by its flaws. A corrupt mayor, an overeager police force, things the world really takes note of. Play your cards right, and you might even get terrorism. All the interesting places have scars on them. And I like to think my village does, too.

Yes, I have both a bakery and a chocolate shop. The public school is obviously well funded. Families are carolling, and judging by the Sold Out! sign, the local theatre is doing surprisingly well. But I also have a hockey rink upon which one of the players is missing an arm. Most people would've thrown the piece away. At the very least, the glue gun would've come out. But I welcomed the change. Overnight, mine became the only Christmas village I know of to have a kid whose arm was chewed off by a wheat thresher.

I've got a horse with a chipped ankle who is unaware that he's being trotted back to the stable to be shot. There's a bridge with a cracked foundation. There's a house with a blinking light: the tenants can't afford the unregulated cost of coal, and it's going to be a long winter.

And it's not just the pieces that have had a hard off-season that add an element of realism. I've started shopping for pieces that lend themselves to unfortunate backgrounds. There's a woman looking out a hotel window and thinking of jumping. There's a man feeding ducks, forlorn because he's in love with his brother-in-law. There's a chimney sweep who looks like shit and should've unionized years ago but instead drinks his paycheque and goes home to a wife who doesn't love him and kids who don't respect him. Wolves lurk in the Christmas tree lot.

"Excuse me," I once asked a clerk in Moncton's Winter Wonderland Park as I held up a small hydrant. "Do you have any buildings that are actually on fire?"

Mine is not a village that keeps the joy of the season in its heart the whole year round.

Mine is a city that understands the true weight of mortality—its fleeting and fragile nature—and has grown accustomed to closed-casket funerals. Mine is a city that embraces the true spirit of Christmas only because its citizens so desperately need a holiday from the lifelong process of dying.

This past summer, Litia drove Maisy and me to New York. Since we could stay with her friend, she promised that little to no money would be spent. As we wandered around the low-rises of Brooklyn, we stumbled across a Yule Tides store. "What luck," I said. Litia sighed and said she'd wait outside with the dog.

I was surprised to be greeted by a cashier who was the same age as me, his face covered with piercings and a thick beard. He nodded as I walked to the back.

I was lost in the world of the village, enamoured with the seafood shop's surprisingly busty waitress, when I realized that the cashier was standing beside me in the otherwise empty store. He leaned back against the table. "Did you know," he began, "that this store used to be a front for bootleggers? And back here was where the dogfighting happened."

I was startled by his honesty. For all he knew, I could've been in there doing early Christmas shopping, or killing time, or looking to see where my demented grandmother had wandered off to. But he could tell that I wasn't. He could tell that my being inside a Yule Tides at 10:30 on a Tuesday morning in May somehow connected with this brutal story.

The cashier's hands outlined where the pit used to be. "Sometimes," he continued, "when a dog was unbeatable, they'd put it up against a man with a baseball bat." As I listened, I found myself coincidentally fidgeting with a figurine of a German shepherd, the breed that Maisy most resembles, and imagined it leaping into blood lust.

For a moment, we both stared at the village, its pristine world untouched by the grim history of the building that housed it.

I waited until I couldn't anymore. "What'd they do with the bodies?"

"The dogs or the humans?" he asked.

"Both."

The bell above the door chimed, and we both turned to see Litia popping her head in, Maisy panting happily beside her. How much longer, she asked. I held up the German shepherd figurine and said I was seeing if he took credit. The cashier nodded, complicit in the lie.

As December gradually descends, Christmas stores welcome their seasonal shoppers, their fair-weather friends. Suddenly, the village section loses its monastic silence as the loved ones of village collectors stumble around, haplessly buying the wrong pieces. I want to tell them that if their grandmothers don't already have a town tree, they are beyond help.

But one year, in a Christmas miracle, Litia got it right. I do all of my holiday shopping months in advance, scoping out the best deals. Litia, however, leaves hers until reindeer hooves are touching the roof. As usual, I wasn't expecting much, hoping for something only slightly better than my father's annual gift card for the Keg (I've been a vegetarian for five years).

I unwrapped a four-inch town clock, and my eyes stung with water. It was something that I didn't even know I needed—a discovered need—and something the village had been blind without. A piece both powerful and understated, something that everything could revolve around. What the sun is to the earth, the clock is to my village. And I would place it beneath the light of my full moon.

But more often than not, village gifts are kind gestures offered by those who have no fucking clue. My mother has bought me two churches in the past two years, decimating my tax base. My friend Lindsay got me an ice cream shop. Why would you have an ice cream shop in a town that is locked in eternal winter? For some questions, there are no answers.

By far the worst piece, though, was from my brother. It was the first Christmas after we had put down our family dog, Buddy. I was fifteen at the time, Tress a year older. He got me a figurine of a woman opening a wrapped box while a man watches behind her. Inside the box, a dog pants happily. Tress thought this piece would remind me of Buddy each year when I set up my village.

There are two things I hate about this piece. First, both the woman and the man are wearing Gore-Tex jackets. Second, it is completely improbable. That dog is lucky to be alive. It isn't panting because it's happy but because nobody bothered to poke air holes in the box.

Why do I keep such horrendous pieces? Because you can either be small and perfect like Monaco and sit in the back of the room during international dealings, or you can be colossal and hungry like the Soviet Union and watch the sun set on one end of your empire only to see it rise on the other.

I know that many things about my relationship with the village seem illogical: the sweatshop tolerance, the fiscal foolishness, the fact that I don't even really like Christmas. What can I say? Picasso's cubism, Eliot's modernism, Gandhi's view of the human soul—each, in its way, disconnected from logic. But that is what happens when you try to create something beautiful in an unbeautiful world.

I've never asked Litia what she thinks of the village, but not out of fear that she would say something mean. My dread is that she'd say she loves it because it is the one thing that makes me human: my tender and nonsensical affection.

As for her saying she hates it, that's not even possible. She's too weak for hate, though she would say too strong.

I want to give her everything this side of the solar system, but the only lives I can offer her right now are the ones barely worth having—hard and rigid, delicate and inflexible. We've started to talk about having a kid, and I become paralyzed with fear of what those sticky fingers will do to my empire. But I'm also afraid that I'll be heartbroken when Litia loves this new thing more than she loves me. And the two of them will be living their lives in so large a fashion, while I'll be trapped inside, keeping company with my petty fears, looking out at them through my teeny little window.

I should admit that mine is not the largest village in the world. Not even close. Like most of my boyhood dreams, the Internet has destroyed that illusion. Eighty-nine-year-old Milt Hildebrant from Mendota Heights, Minnesota, is famous for a superstate that slinks through fully two rooms of his bungalow. It is an 1,100-piece collection, many times larger than my own.

I once took solace in the belief that, at least in Canada, I was a big fish in a small polyresin duck pond. But in March 2015, a major Christmas village brand posted a photo on its Facebook page of a deceptively modest ten-piece set. The buildings are spaced out, the streets peppered with people. There is a pastry store and a jeweller. There is a portrait painter on the corner and a wooden fence that encircles a merry-go-round. But what caught my eye was the moon, the same one as mine, its treasonous face glowing with pride.

Usually, I would've met the photo with pity, even outright derision. But the caption beneath the photo sent shivers down my spine: it explained that the builder of the village was a Canadian teenager.

When I was fourteen, my set had only seven pieces, one being my hockey team with nineteen arms. This kid had just a handful of buildings last year, and you can tell by the way he talks that he's got big city plans. If his village progresses at the rate I expect, this kid will surely overtake me by his twenty-fifth birthday. I needed to know: Who is this prodigy? And thanks to his shockingly relaxed Facebook security settings, I was able to find out.

He is indeed a teenager, and owing to a post he made about his report card, I know he is an excellent student. I know that he's into cake decorating in a big way. I know he likes bike riding; I know his older sister is a total babe and his father rocks sunglasses in formal portraiture. And also, because of a sickeningly sweet photo of the family in their front yard, I know that he lives nearby.

I think back to my teenage self and all the money I wasted on comic books and guinea pig food and trying to date girls who were obviously never going to go out with a boy who revered the key differences between ceramic and porcelain.

My young rival's village has perfect aesthetic balance; mine has villagers who can't even keep their arms attached to their bodies.

He is coming for me. And his part-time job is only hurrying things along. My wasted time, my wasted life.

If I had the courage to reach out to him, what would I say? I would say that, for the rest of his life, people will tell him a miniature Christmas village is a childish thing. But I would also tell him that the people who say this have no appreciation for the finer things, for the small flourishes of beauty—and that, when you get right down to it, they don't know shit about the fragility of the human heart. I would also tell him that they are 100 percent correct.

But adulthood is nothing to write home about. Yes, it's true that there are credit cards and cigarettes, which are pretty great. It's also true that people will stop being embarrassed when you ask them to explain the lyrics of "Hotel California." You can get a dog; you can watch *The Godfather*, parts one and two. There's no point in lying; there is a lot to be said for being a big person.

But then you'll keep growing to the point where you no longer grow, and you are what you are, and the oyster-shaped world adults promised you will be revealed as a preamble to their pyramid scheme, something they'd stupidly bought into and now need you to as well. There's nothing wrong with wishing for a different world. But one day, wishes won't matter—or rather, you'll realize they never mattered and were just one of the Santa Claus lies told to you by parents, teachers, and the elderly obese. By then, the end of the merge lane will have cornered you, and you'll have to weave yourself into the traffic, seat-belted into unfathomable speed; but you'll still wish for a perfection so still and silent, like rainbow trout in a frozen-through lake. My greatest fear? That this world will pass me over like I would a miniature man in a top hat, like something it has seen 1,000 times already and will see 10,000 times more.

But of course I'll never say this. There's only so much you can put in an unsolicited email to an adolescent boy.

My brother, my parents, and Litia are all drinking eggnog at the kitchen counter, Maisy curled up at their feet. I am alone in the dining room. The stereo switches CDs and "Carol of the Bells" comes on, building to its crescendo. My pillars of boxes are empty; my hand is still hovering the plug's prongs over the socket. In the bay window, I catch my reflection, hunched and scowling and shrouded in darkness. But the plug enters the socket and suddenly I am bathed in light as power surges through my fingers and into my streets, the banks of lampposts like an airstrip guiding me home. The frozen eyes of my villagers are bright with desire; their houses are consumed by radiance. My theatre, my hotel, my millinery: All of it shines with a light so bright, it is pure colour. An apocalyptic fire. And above it all is my moon, now shrill with operatic pain.

Here I am, surrounded by my city and its inhabitants, feeling like a god. And I bless them, every one.

White Matter
Susan Olding

Slug: a slow, lazy person. A sluggard.

LEAVING THE COTTAGE, the girl pushes the screen door as far as it will go, just to be sure that it will spring back with a satisfying smack. She does not look behind her, does not turn to see her mother's frown or the embittered twist of her gingham tea towel. She does not look because it serves her mother right. *Get out, get out. Quit lying around, for god's sake. Put away that book and go!*

The ground, knotted with pine roots and slippery with their needles, slopes towards a narrow estuary. Down there, on the floating dock, the girl's little brother pokes in the brackish water with a net, looking for eels. If he catches any her father will cook them on the hibachi for supper. She shudders. It's not that she's squeamish. Spiders, ants, wasps, mice, land snakes, tadpoles, toads, even the pickled brains in the lab where her father works— these she can look on with composure and even curiosity. But the thought of touching a live eel or any creature composed of slime sickens her.

She turns from the water and heads for the fields, tucking up the hem of her skirt. A maxi, sewn for a project in Home Economics class, it's a swathe of white cotton with an elastic waistband and a wide eyelet ruffle at its bottom. Years from now, she'll reject this style for its tendency to make grown women look like little girls, but now she's convinced that her ground-sweeping skirt transforms her into someone taller and older than her twelve years. And that is why she wears it as often as she can, even though she hates the way it trips her up when she walks.

Past the stand of pines, she crosses a gravel road and leaps a ditch. At last, she comes to the grasses, waist-high, sweet smelling, home on this sunny afternoon to grasshoppers and blackbirds and hundreds of yellow butterflies. Here, the sunlight scrubs the air to a transparent sheen; here, a stray breeze carries the musk of wild rose and the tang of salt. She breathes, brushes dried lichen from a large, low stone, spreads her skirts around her, and pulls the offending book from the pocket of her kangaroo sweater. It serves her mother right.

As she reads the afternoon away, the girl does not understand the difficulty of the task she is engaged in. She does not know her brain never evolved to read, does not know that to do so, it must "recycle" its related powers of visual and gestural recognition and connect these to its faculties for coding speech sounds and making meaning; she does not know that the cognitive, linguistic, and perceptual hoops she must jump in order to synchronize all these skills are so improbable and astonishing that one day they will be likened to a neurological "three-ring circus." She only knows that she isn't, as her mother seems to believe, a slothful and lazy person. She only knows that her mother, as usual, is wrong.

Slug: a slow sailing vessel.
The book she reads is *Oliver Twist*. She hasn't seen the movie, hasn't seen the stage play. She pulled this paperback from a shelf at her local Coles because it stood at the back with the "Classics" and she thought it was a book for grownups.

Oliver Twist is a child. But it takes some effort to enter his world. The first few chapters are slow going. Reading this book is not like reading the teen magazines she gorges on back in the cabin; it's not like reading her schoolbooks, or her favourite kids' books, or the daily newspaper, or the backs of the cereal boxes. So at times—not that she'd admit this—she does not understand what's going on. She's young, after all, and she lacks context. The novel first appeared 150 years ago, and much about the world has changed. Perched on her stone near Boothbay Harbor, Maine, she is 3,000 miles away from London, a fabled city she has never seen. And though she wants more than anything to be treated as an adult, she knows—oh, she knows, though she cringes to admit it—she is almost as naïve and "green" as her book's eponymous hero.

Why, she wonders, is Fagin always called "the Jew"? Why does the Dodger laugh so hard at Oliver, and what do his slang expressions mean? Who is Monks? Who was Oliver's mother and what did she do wrong? And what, exactly, is going on between Sikes and Nancy?

Years from now, the girl will learn that she is not the only reader to be confused by this novel's peculiar blend of irony and social commentary and gothic horror. She'll find out that its youthful author wrote it without a significant plan and at a breakneck pace to satisfy public demand. She will wince at Dickens' sentimental portraits of women and children, even as she marvels, like so many others, at the psychological depth and strange appeal of some of his ostensible villains.

By then, neuroscientists will claim that emotionally compelling narratives light up the anterior insula and the mid-cingulate cortex—the affective empathy networks of the brain—while more neutral passages do not. They'll argue that descriptions of a protagonist's pain or personal distress activate these core structures, and the higher the proportion of empathy-inducing elements in a story, the higher a reader's tendency to become immersed or "lost" in that book. Perhaps this helps to explain the perennial appeal of Charles Dickens.

But all the girl knows now is that when Nancy steals Oliver from his kindly protectors, she loses track of time. All she knows is that she isn't aware of her surroundings—doesn't hear the blackbirds calling, doesn't taste the salt on the air, doesn't feel the heat of the sun or the roughness of the rock. Reading this story transports her. It makes her feel like one of those boats she's watched while waiting for her parents to buy groceries down in Boothbay Village. The way they speed sometimes toward the open sea, wind billowing their sails. The way they waft and glide, their lazy drift a mark of splendid privilege.

Slug: some kind of strong drink.
Her mother shouldn't preach. She's the one who can't stop reading. Stacks of books back home, as tall as these grasses; even here, on vacation, the first place she visited in town was the public library. She's just mad because she has to make the meals and do the washing up; she's just mad because she likes to nurse her novels alone, and unless the girl goes out, that isn't possible.

Is reading a weakness? Is it an addiction, like smoking and gambling and drinking? And if so, could it be inherited? It might be, the girl suspects, it might be. Because why else is it so hard for her to stop? Blind now to her book's faults—its creaking, implausible plot; its cipher of a hero; its melodramatic highs and lows; its inconsistencies and caricatures—she's snagged by its broad satire; held by the humour of its dialogue; rocked by the rhythms of its sentences; caught in the painful predicaments of its characters. The sun beats down, setting the black print to dance on the blazing pages. She rubs her eyes, blinks at the bright white paper, and reads on.

The girl doesn't know it, but her mother's admonitions spring from a venerable tradition. Ever since Socrates, reading has provoked ambivalence in those responsible for children's education. Ever since Socrates, the fear that young people might read "too much" or "the wrong thing" has been a source of public alarm. Reading's been accused of supplanting memory and promoting the pretence of wisdom. It's been compared to the use of opium and called a compulsion and contagion, the "source of all moral corruption" and a fount of "savagery." Fiction, in particular, has aroused the concern of certain parties. Women from every class and station of life have been scolded for their love of novels, which have been blamed for inflaming their emotions, stirring their senses, breeding romantic daydreams, sparking radical ideas, and disappointing them in reality. Not to mention: ruining their eyes, their posture, and their work habits. "Without this poison instilled, as it were, into the blood, females in ordinary life would never have been so much the slaves of vice."

By the time the girl is grown, much anxiety will revolve around the act of reading on the Internet. In China and Korea, people at computers will forget to eat, forget to sleep, neglect to defecate. In Internet cafés, they will drop dead by the dozen, and some psychiatrists will push to include the designation "Internet Addiction" within the Fifth Edition of the Diagnostic and Statistical Manual of Mental Disorders, their profession's bible.

By then, people who say they are addicted to books as opposed to screens will claim this status ironically or as a badge of honour. Novels will be viewed as quaint and harmless (at worst) or improving (at best); neurobiologists will crow about their lasting and positive effects on the language centres of the brain. But now, the Internet does not exist; functional magnetic resonance imaging has yet to be adopted. And the dopamine hit that floods the girl's brain is the strongest she has ever known. The strongest she can imagine.

Slug: a heavy or hard blow; a beating.

There are few passages in English literature as well known as the murder of Nancy. At seven pages out of total of 415, the chapter called "Fatal Consequences" packs a punch far in excess of its mere proportion. The deed itself takes little more than a paragraph to describe. The robber, Sikes, believing himself betrayed, hauls his lover, Nancy, from her bed, beats her with the butt of his pistol, and then bludgeons her for good measure. Before he strikes her, she begs him to spare her and prays to God for mercy. But spare her Sikes will not. He hits, and hits, and hits again, until her hair clings to his club and her blood splatters his clothing, until her blood soaks the walls and the floors, until the very feet of his dog are steeped in blood.

In Dickens' day, and for 150 years thereafter, this chapter was mostly dismissed as the lowest melodrama. Most adaptations of the story shrink from portraying its full brutality. But recent research suggests that the scene was based on fact. Only months before Dickens finished his manuscript, one Eliza Grimwood was killed in a similar fashion. Like Nancy, Eliza was a prostitute; like Nancy, she was taken from her bed; like Nancy, she was forced to her knees. The case was notorious at the time, and Dickens certainly knew of it.

His own version of the story was a source of pride to him. After he wrote it, he showed it to his wife, Catherine. She fell into an "unspeakable *state*," from which he "auger[ed] well." His faith in the material lingered. Long after he'd finished *Oliver Twist*—his first, apprentice novel—its criminal characters kept their hold on him. Some thirty years later, overriding the objections of some of his friends and associates, he took to performing the scene in public. Acting out the four principal parts in turn, he is said to have embodied these characters so thoroughly that he became them. His friend, Charles Kent, reported:

Whenever he spoke [as Fagin], there started before us—high-shouldered with contracted chest, with birdlike claws, eagerly anticipating by their every movement the passionate words fiercely struggling for utterance at his lips—that most villainous old tutor of young thieves, receiver of stolen goods, and very devil incarnate: his features distorted with rage, his penthouse eyebrows (those wonderful eyebrows!) working like the antennae of some deadly reptile, his whole aspect, half-vulpine, half-vulture-like, in its hungry wickedness…As for the Author's embodiment of Sikes—the burly ruffian with thews of iron and voice of Stentor—it was only necessary to hear that infuriated voice, and watch the appalling blows dealt by his imaginary bludgeon in the perpetration of the crime, to realise the force, the power, the passion, informing the creative mind of the Novelist at once in the original conception of the character, and then, so many years afterwards, in its equally astonishing representation.

Every time Dickens staged the murder, some of his spectators would become hysterical. After one such reading, he claimed to have had "a contagion of fainting; and yet the place was not hot. I should think we had from a dozen to twenty ladies taken out stiff and rigid at various times!" Nor were the audience members alone in feeling the effects of his performance. At nearly sixty, his health was frail. His family worried about him. At their insistence, he hired doctors to stand by at his public readings. In checking, they discovered that as he threw himself, body and soul, into the violent action, his pulse would race as high as 112 beats per minute. Later, some of his loved ones would blame his enthusiastic and repeated presentations of this story for hastening his stroke and early death.

Dickens, his friends, and his audiences intuitively understood what neuroscientists would not discover for another century:

reading heightens connectivity in the central sulcus or the primary sensory motor region of the brain. To put it another way: thinking about running activates the neurons associated with the physical act of running. So, by extension, reading about beating someone activates the neurons associated with actually beating someone. Perhaps the age-old fears about the dangers of reading have some basis in neurobiology, after all.

But perched on her lichen-spotted rock near the shores of Maine, the girl, who has finished the fateful chapter, is ignorant of this. All she knows is that her palms hurt from the pressure of her nails, her gut feels tight, her heart pounds hard—and suddenly, she's chilled to the bone. She looks up. The sun has slipped behind the line of evergreens. The sky is turning lavender. The hem of her skirt is damp. She must have missed supper. Did her mother call? If so, she didn't hear. And by this time, her mother will be furious. Half-dazed, frightened, resentful, guilty, she shuts her book, stretches her arms, wiggles her toes—and screams.

Slug: a slow-moving, slimy gastropod; a caterpillar or larva.
All around her, everywhere, on each blade of grass, and every leaf of every flower, are slugs. Fat, greyish white, an inch or more in length, and slimy, they surround her. No matter where she turns— at ground level, at eye level, at all levels—they're everywhere. Their greasy flesh glistens in the gloom. Worse, they are *moving*, moving slowly, but moving ever closer, nearer to her hands, her heart, her head, whatever parts of her comprise her *self*. Dozens cling to the trim of her ridiculous skirt. One of them is crawling onto her leg.

Is it the slugs or the story that scare or scar her so?

Slug: a counterfeit coin.
The brain science of Charles Dickens' day was phrenology. Phrenologists believed that the mind was composed of multiple,

distinct, and innate faculties, and that each faculty was represented by a separate "organ" of the brain, which occupied a specific area. They thought the size of these organs roughly corresponded to their relative power, and that each could be enhanced or controlled through an effort of the will. To determine the size and shape of the various organs, they studied the shapes (or the "bumps") of people's skulls. Did a person's "sense of cunning" overbalance her "good nature or compassion"? Did he show a "disposition for colouring and delighting in colours" or a "sense for sounds"? Or perhaps she was blessed a highly developed "mechanical skill" or "wit." In total, there were thought to be anywhere from twenty-six to thirty-three of these faculties, and their relative weight in a person's brain could help explain that person's character and suggest directions for cultivation or pruning with the goal of self-improvement.

Phrenology's influence on nineteenth-century life and culture was immense. The reasons are not so mysterious. An apparently testable process that promised answers to the riddle of self-knowledge, it seemed to offer a path towards personal growth and social control. Eventually, its jargon and central principles wound their way into almost every branch of thought, including anthropology, education, criminology, medicine, and of course the arts.

Dickens, like many of his peers, was generally sympathetic to phrenology. He often used its language as a kind of shorthand for his characters' dispositions, and its influence extended to his real life decisions. In 1847, he refused to admit a woman to Urania Cottage, the home for "fallen women" that he'd co-founded and helped to operate, on the grounds of her phrenology. "She had a singularly bad head, and looked discouragingly secret and moody."

But he was less convinced when his own skull was the subject of scrutiny. In *Martin Chuzzlewit*, he mocked the "American frenzy" to examine his head—perhaps annoyed by one commentator's insistence that a plaster bust of his likeness offered proof of a common-place, even mediocre mind. "*Boz* is no doubt amusing–very amusing, for an occasional hour," but "[t]he fact itself, of an author's productions being so extensively read and admired, and that too even amongst uneducated persons, proves them adapted to the ordinary taste and intelligence rather than raised far above it."

Slug: a lead bullet.
The bullet that finally shot phrenology dead was scientific rigour. By the end of the nineteenth century, its assumptions were thoroughly discredited. Investigation showed that the contours of the skull had nothing to do with the structure of the brain beneath, thus demolishing one of its core premises. Prominent brain researchers criticized it as a pseudo-science, on the level of astrology, necromancy, and alchemy. Yet the British Phrenological Society did not disband until 1967. And the language of phrenology continued to haunt popular culture long after its official demise.

Ironically, some of phrenology's basic ideas have since been affirmed by neuroscience. We now take for granted the idea that the physiology of the brain can affect behaviour—this is why we see personality changes after a stroke or brain injury. We also accept that certain brain functions, such as language, are localized. And we know that specific areas of the brain can grow in response to stimulus. Take, for instance, the right hippocampus in London cabbies—or cortical thickness in the left hemispheres of children who read for pleasure.

Does this mean that phrenology was right, after all? Of course not. The brain is not a cage of competing traits like "acquisitiveness" and "vanity" and "poetic talent" and "perspicuity." It is the hub of distinctive and dynamic processes, like moving, touching, hearing, smelling, speaking. Phrenology was a mistaken hypothesis that morphed into a kind of mass delusion. But the gun that killed it is a heavy one and casts its own long shadow over contemporary culture.

Slug: a rough pellet.

In phrenology's heyday, it was common to see illustrations of the skull complete with the locations of various traits drawn in. Those who went for phrenological readings could buy ceramic busts of marked-up heads as a kind of souvenir. Today, the tools of neuroscience, including magnetic resonance imagery, functional magnetic resonance imagery, magnetoencephalography, electroenchephalography, positron emission tomography, and near-infrared spectroscopy, provide similarly authoritative-seeming representations of the brain. These images have become ubiquitous in all kinds of contexts and publications, from the abstruse psychology manual to the popular sports magazine. And the "brain science" associated with them is used to rationalize and explain everything from personality quirks and talents, to the effects of stroke or dementia, to the experience of learning a second language or of reading. What, and how much, we eat; how and how often we exercise; whether we should have sex, take up an instrument, play computer games, do crossword puzzles, read nonfiction on the Internet or novels for pleasure—all of this comes down to the (supposed) effects of these activities on our brain. As if—to return to another discredited theory, even older than phrenology—the brain were a kind of homunculus.

Critics argue that neuroscience has become our own generation's dominant mythology. They point out that many of its studies are poorly designed, statistically meaningless, badly controlled, carelessly written, or misappropriated to justify false and damaging stereotypes. Others claim that its tools, particularly neuroimaging, are less reliable than often admitted, and its findings, even when valid, still require a depth of reflective interpretation that is often lacking in the reports.

As with phrenology, the rhetoric of "brain power" fills us with mingled hope and despair. It pledges that, if only we can locate the various functions of the brain and learn how best to exercise them, we can improve ourselves. Perhaps we can become better parents, lovers, learners. Perhaps we can eliminate depression, Alzheimer's, reading disability. Who wouldn't wish for that? Yet the promise is fraught, for if our problems persist even in the face of continual "brain training," we risk the censure or disdain of others and may feel inadequate, out of control, and ashamed.

Neuroscience has taught us much that unravels the workings of the human brain and helps us respond to genuine human needs. But even its practitioners warn that it can be baldly reductive. And in a culture gone mad for brain-based explanations, the question is whether the language of neuroscience tells us anything we don't already know—anything that artists have not already articulated and explored with far greater richness and power. In observing a girl racing headlong through a field, a neuroscientist could, with confidence, note that the sensorimotor functions of her brain were highly active, and equally could point to the place where those reside. Just so, a phrenologist, examining the skull of a man like Sikes might remark upon his highly developed faculty for "murder and carnivorousness." The neuroscientist would speak with greater truth—but arguably, less significance.

Memory not only is *like* fiction; it *is* fiction. So say the neuroscientists—and the novelists before them. Flying through the slug-infested field, stumbling across the gravel road, panting, half-blind with worry and fear, the girl finally reaches the swaying pines and stops for a moment to remove a rough pellet from her sandal. She bends, and her book slides out of her pocket. It lands, face up, open to one of Cruikshank's most famous illustrations. *Oliver, asking for More.*

Slugline: an identifying title.

For years, neuroscientists focused their research on the grey areas of the cerebral cortex, locating and then teasing out the characteristics of numerous distinct functions, including planning, problem solving, vision, balance, and co-ordination, which in some ways resemble the old "traits" so beloved of phrenologists.

But the brain moves remarkably fast for an organ with the consistency of a slug. It learns, adapts, expands, creates. It can invent an enduring story that evokes a world for someone thousands of miles and hundreds of years away; it can read that story and grow, in the course of a few afternoons, from a gormless larva of a girl to a creature endowed with wings. None of this could occur without a means of communication between the areas that control reason, emotion, language, movement, and memory. None of this could occur without an intricate network of connections.

White matter is the stuff that makes it possible.

Dr. Shock
Richard Poplak

INSPECTED FROM ABOVE, there is nothing—just the converging serpents of the Limpopo and Shashe Rivers, and a plateau surrounded by endless tracts of veld. In 1970, a military camp was built here, overseen by a psychiatrist who believed firmly in the curative power of pain. In apartheid's darkest corners, he was known as die Kolonel, his camp was christened Greefswald, and no two terms inspired more dread in the members of the South African Defence Force, themselves experts in the creation and dissemination of terror.

Hundreds of white teenage boys were processed through Greefswald in the 1970s, and its survivors still drift through the country like ghosts. I recently met one, who insisted I refer to him only by his Hebrew name, Itiel. He was born in 1951, he told me, and in his teens succumbed to the Aquarian drug warp. Through a scrim of hallucinogens, he watched the apartheid regime congeal around him. "I was basically psychotic," he said. "I felt as though I'd come to a strange planet."

South Africa in the '60s was the strangest planet. The Sharpeville massacre, in which the regime killed sixty-nine unarmed black protesters, served as the decade's bloody opening allegro. Black opposition parties were banned, dissenters filled the prisons, and in 1964 Nelson Mandela was sentenced to a life term. Two years later, Prime Minister Hendrik Verwoerd, the so-called architect of apartheid, was stabbed to death by a parliamentary messenger who claimed to take orders from a tapeworm in his stomach. As if serving the same parasite, the government introduced universal conscription in 1967. Almost every white male in his late teens was churned through the SADF's meat grinder, and if any failed to emerge as "normal," he was processed again until he did.

Itiel's conscription papers ordered him to a Pretoria drill hall in January 1971. For a habitual drug user quitting cold turkey, basic training made for a cruel comedown. He committed a near-fatal error: after deciding that he no longer wanted to be in the military, he informed a solicitous officer about his substance abuse. A week or so later, without warning or explanation, he was sent to 1 Military Hospital, or 1 Mil, the SADF's sprawling medical campus in Pretoria. Within its austere fortifications lurked the psychiatric wards, infamous throughout the army as the loony bin, the nuthouse, the abyss within the abyss. Military psychiatric hospitals were first established to mend minds damaged by war, but only a few of the wards' inmates had experienced combat. Instead, about half the forty beds were occupied by gays, rock 'n' rollers, and dope heads—the counterculture's ragged foot soldiers. "They were most interested in what songs we listened to," a former patient named Gordon Torr told me. "What they feared most were people who didn't think the way they did."

The wards were die Kolonel's domain. He was everywhere and nowhere, a god but not a benevolent one. It was understood that he subjected homosexuals to shock treatment in order to straighten them out. But there were also whispers of palliative circle-jerk sessions in which the psychiatrist allegedly participated. The showers were often splattered with semen, and the enormous doses of psychotropics only enhanced the wards' purgatorial edge. "There was just this feeling," Torr said. "A loss of innocence, suddenly, when you realized there was a dark subculture of sexual perversity."

When Itiel was summoned for a consultation, he found that die Kolonel was not the bogeyman he expected but a stout thirty-two-year-old with sharp eyes and a waistline so considerable that it had earned him a second, more derisive nickname: Bubbles. The doctor performed a Rorschach test and asked his new patient to fill out several questionnaires. Then die Kolonel—properly known as Aubrey Levin, rank of colonel, SADF psychiatrist principal grade—uttered the words that, by almost any measure, proved to be Itiel's death sentence.

"To get to the essence of who you are," he said, "we are going to peel you like an onion."

Several days later, Itiel was loaded onto a Bedford truck and driven north to Greefswald, near the Zimbabwe and Botswana borders. No one in his family was contacted, and no one outside of a select few in the SADF knew where he was going. He was now a subject in a social experiment led by Levin in his capacity as the military's head shrink—one of many brutal psychiatric ventures that, over the course of nearly half a century, would destroy innumerable lives on two continents. Four decades later, Levin would be convicted in Calgary for the sexual abuse of three male patients—although there were likely scores of other victims. The newspapers would call him Dr. Shock, a reference to his history of applying non-consensual shock therapy to gay SADF recruits. No one stopped him during apartheid; no one stopped him during South Africa's transition to democracy in 1994; no one stopped him in Canada until 2010. How did this happen? How was Levin granted a comfortable career in his adoptive home, protected by its medical colleges—all when he had such unambiguous ties to one of the twentieth century's most loathsome regimes?

These questions would only occur to Itiel much later. In July

1971, rattling around in the back of that Bedford, he was just another link in a chain that would eventually bind him to countless young men in Alberta. All were as vulnerable and broken as he was, and all were victims of an ancient and remarkably persistent trope: the monster disguised in the robes of a healer.

Aubrey Levin was born in Johannesburg on December 18, 1938. "The first things you've got to understand about Levin are that (a) he's Jewish and (b) he comes from not just an unusual Jewish family, but one that may have been unique in South Africa," a forensic psychiatrist named Robert M. Kaplan told me. A South African now based at the University of Wollongong, in Australia, Kaplan has followed Levin's career for almost two decades. The Levins, he said, were devout right-wing racists, and they existed on the fringes— boxing promoters, tombstone carvers. This made them unsuitable Shabbat table companions, so they looked elsewhere to belong. Although the ruling, largely Afrikaner National Party maintained a clause excluding Jews from membership, the Levins nonetheless managed to graduate from outspoken apartheid apologists to card-carrying nationalists, their prospects for advancement improving as they did so.

Overweight, bookish, and brilliant, Levin graduated from high school at fifteen, and in 1956 he signed up to study medicine at the University of Pretoria on an SADF scholarship. His ambition was relentless. He acted as foreign correspondent for the university newspaper, chaired the university's Student Jewish Association, vice-chaired the SA Federation of Students' Jewish and Zionist Associations, and helped run the Coordinating Committee of University Societies. None of these exertions took the edge off his politics. He was known to break up meetings of leftists and communists, hurling chairs and ripping down posters. While blacks came in for plenty of opprobrium, Levin hated nothing more than dope smokers and gays—cohorts he routinely conflated.

By 1966, he was treating patients with acute mental disorders at Johannesburg General Hospital. International watchdogs considered South Africa's psychiatric institutions dumping grounds for the regime's black opponents. While this was certainly true in isolated cases, black dissidents were by no means the target demographic. "After 1939," writes Tiffany Fawn Jones in *Psychiatry, Mental Institutions, and the Mad in Apartheid South Africa,* "institutions and practitioners focused on the very people that the apartheid government wanted to uplift—poor white men."

But how to define madness in a country that itself displayed all the symptoms of collective psychosis? Levin devised an answer: no member of white society, regardless of how deviant, was beyond the normalizing power of modern psychiatry. In 1968, he submitted a letter to the secretary of the South African parliament, asking to pitch conservative legislators on a treatment program that would rehabilitate gays and lesbians. "The problem of sexual deviation," he wrote, "requires re-evaluation; without encouraging an unnatural extention [sic] of this problem, it would be better contained and treated by the doctor (rather than by imprisonment)."

Levin didn't believe in criminalizing deviancy out of existence. Rather, he believed in medicating it into oblivion. Early in his career, he researched the effects of Lorazepam, Diazepam, Maprotiline— the psychotropic era's unguided bombs. He was also an enthusiastic proponent of electroshock therapy. His clinical obsession, even more so than homosexuality, was the eradication of marijuana use in the SADF. His doctoral thesis, "An Analysis of the Use of Drugs and Certain Sequelae Thereof with Emphasis on *Cannabis sativa* in a Sample of Young Men Conscripted for Military Service," was considered by the head of the South African Medical and Dental Council an "original and important contribution to the psychiatric field of drug addiction."

In 1967, he married a young university research assistant named Erica, who hailed from Rhodesia (now Zimbabwe). Over the course of Levin's life, Erica would provide unfailing support, not just as a wife and mother but also as an on-hand typist and dogsbody. At what would prove to be enormous personal risk, she remained in awe of her husband until the very end. Together they raised four children, and if their Judaism held them back from becoming model members of the volk, it barely showed.

Two years after marrying, still enlisted in the SADF and under the supervision of Surgeon General Colin Cockcroft, Levin began to design a program that would implement his earlier recommendations to the government. Along with a number of other doctors who helped the regime medicate difference and pathologize dissent, he now had the full might of the South African military-medical complex behind him. He got to work immediately.

Levin's primary innovation was the establishment of a treatment pipeline that extended from 1 Mil in Pretoria to Greefswald in the scorching northern bush. The SADF's wayward boys (and, later, girls) were flagged by commanding officers, chaplains, or medical staff and processed through 1 Mil's psych wards. There, in a highly insular environment, Levin "fixed" inmates' sexuality and other deviances with a combination of drugs and electroshock equipment. Those who didn't fit this treatment profile, or who refused to co-operate, were sent to Greefswald, which die Kolonel began to oversee after Cockcroft installed him at 1 Mil. If his methods were grotesque and unethical, he was the regime's ranking psychiatrist, so it hardly mattered.

No account lays bare the extent of Levin's sway more comprehensively than a document called *The aVersion Project*. Subtitled "Human rights abuses of gays and lesbians in the South African Defence Force by health workers during the apartheid era," compiled by activists and academics, and published in October 1999, it is a multidisciplinary text that reads like Dostoevsky. The report took its cue from South Africa's controversial Truth and Reconciliation Commission process. Convened in 1995, the TRC was meant to cauterize apartheid's suppurating wounds: if the country had any hope of overcoming its past, the reasoning went, then its people needed to hear testimony from both the victims and the perpetrators of the regime's atrocities. The TRC offered certain perpetrators amnesty in exchange for information. Most of those called to the commission came before their fellow citizens to confess their crimes and cast around in the carnage for forgiveness. Levin was not among them.

One TRC submission, compiled by the Health and Human Rights Project and titled *Professional Accountability in South Africa*, implicated twenty-four doctors in human-rights abuses, with Levin making the cut for his torture of SADF recruits at 1 Mil. The TRC proved that regime-doctor complicity was coded into apartheid's operating system, and *The aVersion Project* was an attempt to challenge this hierarchy. Levin goes unnamed in its pages, because the terms of its funding forced the compilers to refer to him as the "Psychiatrist" or the "Colonel." But he exists between the lines as its open secret, its Baal.

One of the primary questions posed by the report was whether gay recruits under Levin's supervision consented to conversion therapy or were forced to comply. Shock treatment was a frequently used and much studied method of "averting" patients from engaging in homosexual behaviour, and although it had fallen out of favour in the United Kingdom and the United States by the 1970s, it was hardly a radical practice. It was, however, behavioural psychiatry at its crudest: show patient image of same-sex nude, apply shock; show patient image of opposite-sex nude, withhold shock; and, lo!—"normalcy" emerges from a chrysalis of pain. Needless to say, there was scant scientific evidence to suggest that the procedure worked.

If, as *The aVersion Project* asserts, the shock therapy became excessive, or if the patient resisted, there was little to distinguish treatment from torture. According to testimony from seventeen informants, including patients, family members, and health care professionals, refusing the Colonel was not an option. Recruits did not check themselves in voluntarily; instead, they were channelled into the wards by authority figures. One such recruit, identified as Clive, told the researchers how the Colonel had claimed that there was nothing to fear from shock treatment, and that he'd used the procedure himself to cure a "predilection for chocolate bon-bons." Clive saw things otherwise. "It kind of like twisted the muscle," he told the researchers. "And then when you kind of reached the maximum point, and then you'd say 'No, no, no, I couldn't stand it any more' then he would say, 'Now you must think about your girlfriend.'" An intern psychologist named Trudie Grobler told the researchers that she once witnessed a lesbian recruit shocked with so much force that her shoes blew off. "I couldn't believe that her body could survive it all," Grobler said.

The report included other accusations. "My first experience with the Colonel," a patient said, "was when he 'checked' my penis for hygiene. I thought that was very unsuitable as his examination had little to do with my mental condition." Levin swamped his patients with medication. Parents were rarely informed. Most recruits cracked; some were broken beyond repair. As one former SADF member told the *The aVersion Project*'s authors, "A chap in our unit couldn't come to terms with the military or his homosexuality, and put his rifle to his mouth and shot himself. Two weeks later, his family [was] notified."

The evidence was overwhelming. The report concluded that inmates "suffered human rights abuses" because they were treated "without proper informed consent. Almost all suffered varying degrees of harm as a consequence of treatment."

And then there was Greefswald. A 1973 United Press International article reported that it was designed "to group addicts together and expose them to the rigors of a fighting military unit." But if at 1 Mil Levin abused conventional psychiatric practice, his camp belonged to a long line of twentieth-century institutions that subscribed to a much darker ideal: *Arbeit macht frei*. Work makes you free.

On arrival, each new boy, or "roofie," was offered his own bespoke welcome. The corpse of a mutilated wild cat was flung onto Gordon Torr's lap; Itiel was pulled from the truck by his hair, a knife against his throat. The boys were dropped into the middle of an Africa they had only encountered in storybooks. Cheetahs and leopards loped beneath acacia, baobab, stinkwood, and buffalo thorn. Shadows revealed themselves to be browsing kudu. Every so often, SADF brass would drive up in Jeeps and Mercedes Benzes for some R and R, drunkenly spraying game with machine-gun fire.

The boys were stripped of their identities the moment they stumbled out of the Bedfords. The first things they lost were their names. They became symbols, and then they became nothing. "The deprivation of food, water, incredible stress and strain we were put under," Itiel told me. "You went through the next threshold, then the next one—then the next one."

They rarely slept, marching through veld, carrying guns with no ammo. Sometimes they worked eighteen hours a day—cracking rocks, digging ditches, building barracks. Contact with their families was forbidden. Violence from the officers begat violence from the other roofies. Itiel worshipped at a big rock in the middle of the camp, supplicating himself before it as the sun rose. "I went back to primal man," he explained. "I saw things there of such mystical meaning, things that were reptilian in myself." There was a term for this in the SADF: *Bosbevok*. Bushfucked.

Every so often, the *wacka-wacka* of a chopper would crack the stillness below Greefswald's plateau, and an SA-330C Puma would disgorge Levin for consultations. When Bubbles arrived, sweating through his khakis, Itiel knew that he and his fellow recruits would be spared hard labour until the doctor returned to Pretoria. In an unbreakable cycle, their tormentor became their saviour became their tormentor. "There are very few people on earth that went through what we went through physically and mentally," Itiel told me. "It was hell."

But the secret could not be contained. Although Levin left the camp's administration in 1974, the death knell was not properly sounded until 1977, when Greefswald's violence spilled over the Botswana border. Three roofies gang-raped a woman, who was eight months pregnant at the time. The attack occurred within full view of her mother and sparked an international incident so serious that even the apartheid government could not cover it up.

After Levin's discharge, he transferred to Addington Hospital, in Durban, where he served as principal specialist and head of the department of psychiatry between 1975 and 1981. He then took a university post in Bloemfontein, followed by a quiet stint as a psychiatry professor at Rhodes University, in Grahamstown, treating patients in a reviled institution called Fort England. His notoriety faded along with his influence. "He had this attitude of, Why would you listen to me? I'm just a big fat frog," a former patient named Sarah Buchner told me.

Nonetheless, like many of his peers, Levin must have known that when apartheid ended, his medical innovations would be recast as his crimes. In 1995, just a year after the inauguration of democracy in South Africa, the doctor and his family evaporated. One day, he was in his rooms at Fort England. The next day, he wasn't. He left in such a rush, claimed his successor, that he didn't even clean out his office. South African justice, blinder than most, would never catch a glimpse of him again.

The Levin family moved to Calgary in 1998 and soon settled in a quiet, leafy neighbourhood in the city's southwest. Aubrey joined the House of Jacob Mikveh Israel synagogue, participating in the familiar rhythms and rituals of Orthodox Judaism, and he became familiar in turn—the obese, devout psychiatrist, an avid reader of non-fiction books and newspapers.

Three years before arriving in Calgary, Levin had moved to Canada and been granted a medical licence based on a dazzling fifteen-page CV he presented to the College of Physicians and Surgeons of Saskatchewan. He quickly became chief of psychiatry at the Regional Psychiatric Centre of Saskatoon, a correctional facility. His resumé read like an inversion of *The aVersion Project*, trumpeting his past as an apartheid-era military psychiatrist, detailing his work with drug users, and quoting proudly the review of his doctoral thesis. The CV made no mention of his conversion program, nor of the camp built near the banks of the Limpopo and Shashe.

Nonetheless, there was more than enough in its pages to give one pause. Had the CPSS investigated Levin more thoroughly, it would have found several black marks on his record after he was discharged in 1974. During his tenure at Durban's Addington Hospital, two complaints were filed with the registrar of the South African Medical and Dental Council. Both concerned invasive physical examinations that accompanied psychiatric consultations. Even when one of the patients later retracted his complaint, his account was disturbing:

He asked me to take off my shoes, socks, and shirt and lie on the examination table...he asked me to pull down my underpants and examined my penis, about which I had complained, he pulled the skin completely back, and then he showed me the redness and the inflammation, asked how it felt. He then took a cream or ointment from a small jar and put it around the inflammation, which aroused me physically, although it was not my intention or Dr. Levine's [sic] intention to do anything which might have been abnormal...

The doctor's eleven-page rebuttal dismissed the accusations as an elaborate conspiracy. In what would emerge as a theme throughout Levin's career, the SAMDC deferred to his power and reputation. "The committee resolved that the explanation of dr [sic] Levin be noted," wrote the registrar, "and that no further action be taken." In an enraged follow-up letter, the other patient's father described the investigation as "quite astonishingly unsatisfactory." Nor were all members of the SAMDC as sanguine as the registrar. "I must express in the strongest terms my objections as a member of the Medical Council," wrote a professor referred to as I. Gordon, "that both cases would seem to have been disposed of."

Dealing with complaints from psychiatric patients constitutes a nearly impossible balancing act: How does an outside arbiter distinguish a lucid grievance from a delusional invention? But in Levin's case, a pattern was taking shape. His most dogged critic was Robert M. Kaplan, the forensic psychiatrist based in Australia. Like Levin, he had grown up in the South African Jewish community and trained as a psychiatrist. Unlike Levin, he had developed an obsession with doctors gone bad and written numerous papers and books on the subject. According to Kaplan, Levin's *pro forma* licensing by the CPSS was typical when it came to overqualified medical practitioners seeking to flee former conflict zones. "I think Levin got into Canada simply because they were looking for well-trained doctors," he told me. "There's always a shortage of psychiatrists, and of course he gave himself a wonderful CV." The Canadian immigration system leans heavily on professional qualifications and experience—the higher the number of points accorded for the applicant's skills, the likelier it is that immigration authorities will rubber-stamp a residency permit.

Levin was also becoming an expert at disappearing. In 1997, he had his name wiped from the SAMDC's register. His last publication was a short essay in a 2004 anthology of psychopharmacology. Referencing only his own work, he wrote an ode to psychotropics called "A Fly on the Wall." By then, he had reinvented himself as a psychopharmacologist and forensic psychiatrist. "My interest," he wrote, "has shifted to borderline personality disorder, risk assessment, management and prevention of violent behaviour." Which meant that, once again, he was given access to an infinite supply of powerless young men—this time in the Canadian correctional system.

If Levin's licensing by the College of Physicians and Surgeons of Saskatchewan can be explained away by provincial naïveté, a desperate need for forensic psychiatrists, and the pre-search engine era, his licensing by the College of Physicians and Surgeons of Alberta presents a much more complicated case. By 1998, the TRC submissions were world famous, and Levin was instantly searchable—and his story was soon making headlines internationally.

Around the time *The aVersion Project* was published, he felt compelled to tell a *Guardian* reporter that at 1 Mil "nobody was held against his or her will. We did not keep human guinea pigs, like Russian communists; we only had patients who wanted to be cured and were there voluntarily." Shortly thereafter, an error-riddled and unverifiable article was published in South Africa's weekly *Mail*

& Guardian, claiming that Levin had forced gender-reassignment surgery on unwilling recruits. (This rumour had been circulating for a long time but was never proven.) The doctor retained Grant Stapon, from the law firm Bennett Jones, who threatened legal action against media outlets that covered the story.

By the mid-2000s, however, the CPSA had received legitimate queries about Levin's past. In 1998, when the college granted him a licence—which he earned without completing a residency or any further training—a doctor with the TRC's Health and Human Rights Project sent the college a letter of concern. He received no reply. In 2003, a film called *Property of the State: Gay Men in the Apartheid Military* was released, featuring an interview with a patient named Michael Smith, who described in detail an electroshock session that Levin oversaw. Kaplan contacted the CPSA, armed with the TRC submissions, *The aVersion Project*, and his own researched, footnoted work. "I got back pretty much a form letter," he told me, "and I understood other people in South Africa got the same letter: 'Dr. Levin didn't fall into our jurisdiction before he came here, and therefore we have no authority in this.' I then tried writing the Canadian Medical Association, and I got lost in a mire of bureaucracy."

The problem is that the medical-college system has a crucial flaw. On the one hand, the CPSA is a self-regulating body empowered by the Health Professions Act to serve "the public by guiding the medical profession." On the other hand, it arguably privileges professionals over the public, because its stakeholders are right up there on the letterhead: physicians and surgeons. Medical colleges play an important role in firewalling doctors from spurious malpractice claims, but self-regulation inevitably slams into the wall of self-interest, and the system tilts toward those who fund it.

At its worst, the system seems like an endless game of whack-a-mole. "Any allegations that we may hear against any physician coming from anywhere are only that: allegations," said Kelly Eby, the CPSA's director of communications and government relations. "We do our best to investigate those within reasonable resources, but until we have proof, it's very difficult to move forward." How the college defines *reasonable resources*, she did not say. And while this would lead an outside observer to assume the CPSA is flooded with sexual impropriety complaints made by unstable patients, forcing the college to be selective about which to investigate, that is not the case. "I would say it's reasonably uncommon," Eby conceded. "If you look at our complaints statistics, sexual-boundary issues are relatively rare, and proving them is even rarer. I would say one to two a year, and not against psychiatrists." The flood, in other words, was barely a trickle; the complaints against Levin did not get lost in a torrent, but a vacuum.

The Bowden Institution, a federal penitentiary, feeds troubled probates to the forensic assessment outpatient service at the Peter Lougheed Centre, one of Calgary's major treatment locations for men moving through the prison system. By 2002, Levin was assessing patients at both facilities, providing them with psychiatric treatment as per judicial order. His choice of specialty put him in contact with men who were in no position to complain about his conduct, since their freedom often depended on positive evaluations.

Lougheed was his primary hunting ground. The most typical—and most fateful—of his prey was a young man who, due to a publication ban, can be identified only as RB. Levin first assessed him in Bowden, following a drunken, near-fatal car crash in 1999. RB had grown up rough—"there were some alcohol issues and substance abuse issues in his family," his lawyer, Richard Edwards, told me—and spent most of his life pinging around the correctional system. Levin was assigned his case and diagnosed the young man with borderline personality disorder. When RB was released on probation in 2002, he entered into Levin's care. According to RB's testimony, that was when the first sexual assault occurred. They continued on and off for eight years.

Levin groomed RB by offering him bus fare, helping him access social assistance, and plying him with so much medication that at one point a pharmacist refused to fill the prescription. As the young man's life unravelled, Levin's influence only increased. In 2006, he was appointed professor of clinical psychiatry at the University of Calgary—despite the fact that Thomas MacKay, Levin's superior at Lougheed, had received at least one boundary violation complaint and asked that a third party be present when Levin conducted physical examinations. (Why a psychiatrist was conducting physical examinations remained a question for another time.) Levin ignored this, just as he ignored requests to conduct sessions with his office door open and to refrain from seeing patients after hours.

RB would sit in his girlfriend's truck before appointments and weep with shame and rage. In one instance, Levin's examinations were so rough that his scrotum began to bleed. The young man understood that there was no point in telling anyone about the doctor's behaviour, because no one in a position of authority would believe him. On the verge of suicide, he purchased a wristwatch spy camera he couldn't afford and wore it into Levin's rooms on two occasions.

The fourteen minutes of footage given to Calgary police in March 2010 told a story much larger than his own. The images revealed a pair of hands, nimble with practice, as they unbuttoned RB's pants and went to work. The sound was inaudible, but, at considerable expense to the Crown, a forensic analyst coaxed meaning from the dissonance:

Levin: That's getting harder, ultimately getting bigger. You can feel it. Just contract it at the bottom as well. That's it. It'll [indiscernible] (clears throat) [indiscernible]. Just try and contract at the balls. There. I'm sure you can see it getting harder.

RB: Mm-hmm.

Levin: And feel it getting harder.

RB: Mm-hmm.

Levin: You could come [indiscernible] already and easier. Can you try coming now? Can you try coming?

When the police arrived at the Levin home on March 23, Erica tried to stop the arresting officer. "Please leave him alone!" she exclaimed. "He was just trying to help those boys!"

Chief crown prosecutor William Wister and his paralegal, Valerie Wallace, make an odd couple. He is thin and stands about six feet five inches tall, while she is rounder and a foot and a half shorter. When the Levin docket landed on their desks in 2010, Wister was based in the Edmonton Crown Prosecutors Office. (Because Levin had so often testified for the Calgary Crown in his capacity as a forensic psychiatrist, the prosecution had to come from elsewhere, to avoid a conflict of interest.) By October 2012, Wister and Wallace, along with a third member of the team, Dallas Sopko, were inhabiting the second floor of the Calgary Delta Hotel, facing off against the doctor and his defence counsel, which was bankrolled by the Canadian Medical Protective Association.

The prosecution had access to hours of police interview tape that depicted Levin as he watched RB's footage, his hands covering his face. He did not apologize or admit guilt, but he told his interlocutor, "Whatever happens, there will be mud on my face. I'm horrified also to the name and the reputation of psychiatry to have somebody charged." It is impossible to decode this statement—to know if it was intended to suggest contrition, a genuine if morally mangled sense of responsibility to uphold the standards of his profession, or if it was merely an acknowledgment that the coming fight would be a hard one.

By then, nearly fifty former patients had come forward. Over the course of what Wallace described as "a very hard few days," the Crown whittled down this group to twenty and then, finally, to nine feasible cases. All of them were troubled, all their stories tragic. One patient would eventually tell the jury that Levin had masturbated him without wearing gloves—a significant detail, since the young man was battling leukemia at the time and was susceptible to infection. "I was so distraughted [*sic*] because of so much medication, I wasn't—I was in—I am in chemo," he testified. "I felt—well, I mean, humiliated."

The defence first moved for a fitness hearing. The submission portrayed Levin as a man in his seventy-third year who was chronically unwell—and the psychiatrist played the part by sitting dead-eyed and slack faced beside his lawyer. "His memory has deteriorated, his concentration," his wife told the judge. "I don't even like to mention it, but he—after he goes to the washroom, often he doesn't do up his zip." The jury dismissed the request, and Levin made a stunning recovery. Supportive colleagues were brought in to attest to the absurdity of a doctor of Levin's stature standing trial. Then the tricks turned dirty. Levin used glaucoma drops to decrease his blood pressure so that he'd be deemed too unwell to stand or so that the trial would be adjourned. He fired his attorney, Alain Hepner, in what seemed like a bid for a mistrial; when the judge refused to call one, he hired the similarly top-drawer Chris Archer.

Once the trial got underway, a perceived hypersensitivity regarding inappropriate touching emerged as the defence's tent pole. While his methods may have seemed irresponsible and abusive to outsiders, his lawyers claimed, Levin was in fact a maverick in a field starved for new ideas. The doctor insisted that his practice was derived from a multidisciplinary grab bag that included psychiatry, urology, and sex therapy. RB's footage, said Levin's legal team, depicted a vastly experienced professional in the act of stimulating the bulbocavernosus reflex, a test that is typically used to gauge the extent of a spinal injury, but that was in this case meant to elicit a behavioural response.

The Crown contended that Levin was not trained as anything other than a psychiatrist, and even there he seemed unwilling to commit himself to anything approaching a recognizable methodology. His records made no mention of his innovative practices; he gave his patients financial assistance; he made comments like "Your wife is lucky" and "You could do damage with that thing." According to Wister, "His defence was that the footage depicted an examination. Ours was that it was sexual assault. Obviously."

As the Crown had anticipated, the defence used the victims' circumstances against them. "There were lots of things to attack them on, in terms of credibility, motivation, reliability," Wallace told me. "So, were they credible witnesses? Did they have some ulterior motive? Which goes to the issue of, how can they accurately report what happened to them?" The jury was confronted with the full extent of the victims' mental decay: when RB testified, he was so agitated that he could not remain sitting and spun around in the witness box. Bizarre behaviour was not restricted to witnesses for the prosecution. Deep into the trial, Erica Levin followed a juror from the courtroom to a transit stop and attempted to buy her off with an envelope of cash. This almost prompted a mistrial, as it was no doubt intended to do. But Wister and Wallace refused to give up. "They just came across the wrong team," Wallace told me. (Erica was found guilty of attempted obstruction and is serving an eighteen-month conditional sentence with house arrest.)

Throughout the proceedings, Levin remained a cypher. He made his way to the court using a walker, Erica by his side, tramping through the snow in a coat that made him seem even bulkier than usual. He did not exclaim or weep.

On January 28, 2013, a jury found Aubrey Levin guilty of three counts of sexual assault. He was found not guilty of two other counts, and the jury was deadlocked on the remaining four cases. He was sentenced to five years in prison, which ended up sticking despite a spirited appeal. The penitentiary itself remains secret, in order to protect his safety.

I last spoke with Itiel at a Johannesburg kosher restaurant called Frangelica's, which serves coffee, blintzes, and cholent to the residents of Glenhazel, the city's Orthodox Jewish enclave. He wore his grey hair and beard wizard-long, and a pair of yellow-tinted aviators implied a close familiarity with psychedelics. He lived nearby, he told me, in an apartment block maintained for the indigent by the Jewish Burial Society.

When Itiel was discharged from Greefswald in July 1972, he found a patch of garden at his family's home and did not move from it for six months. "People used to come down and talk to me, and I didn't know what the hell they were saying," he explained. "You can't relate to anything, can't relate to the future, can't relate to the past. You are, like, *there*. The present only."

Not a trace of Greefswald remains. But many of its ghosts tell a similar story: none survived the journey back to real life intact. Gordon Torr, who managed to build a successful advertising career in the UK, suddenly fell apart a few years ago. He suffered a catastrophic breakdown, became suicidal, and wrote a stunning novelization of his experiences, called *Kill Yourself and Count to 10*. He has come to an intellectual accord with Levin's legacy. "I think of the camp as a metaphor for that peculiarly dark and twisted place in the minds of the people who conceived a pure-white world in which 'otherness' could be dumped like trash into the ghettoes and prisons of apartheid," he told South African *GQ*.

Now that Levin is in prison, has there been any closure—that intangible condition the TRC reached for in the late 1990s? Certainly not for RB, who by September 2014 was broke and homeless. He is now suing Levin, the CPSA, the Calgary police, and the Peter Lougheed Centre in a complicated civil case. The fallen doctor still has his defenders, those who can't—or don't want to—fathom the breadth and depth of his crimes. During sentencing, Jakob Mikveh's Rabbi Yisroel Miller sent a letter pleading for leniency. "The bad does not erase all the good," wrote the rabbi. "I know all the goodness within him still remains. A prison term would be a death sentence for him."

Authoritarian regimes have enlisted numberless medical professionals to treat not the disease in the patient but the patient as the disease. The vast majority of people who come to Canada to work as psychiatrists are committed, well-trained professionals who will never be guilty of malpractice. But the Aubrey Levins of the world, anomalous though they may be, cannot be ignored out of existence. Have Canadian medical colleges become more robust in ensuring that people like him do not enter the system? Kelly Eby told me she wasn't "specifically aware" of any formal process for looking at the history of an applicant's country of origin. *Self-report* remains a key phrase in the CPSA's long list of requirements for those applying for medical licences in Alberta.

A good doctor ends his or her career largely unsung—a cake at a retirement party, a nice obituary in the local paper. A bad doctor destroys hundreds, sometimes thousands, of lives. I spoke with a number of Levin's former patients, and none of them can quite believe that he's in prison. They still fear his reach; they still believe he's out there. Sarah Buchner, who was treated by Levin in Fort England, told me, "All I want is to know that he won't hurt anyone anymore."

As for Itiel, things eventually improved, but not by much. His life never found a track, and he is now dependent on the charity of the Burial Society. "I haven't managed to get back into anything," he said, taking a slug from a can of Coke. "Nobody wants to give me a job." In the final reckoning, he had to concede that Levin had done exactly what he said he'd do—and then some. He'd peeled Itiel like an onion and gotten to the essence of who he was. Then he kept peeling, until there was nothing left at all.

Most Everyone is Mad Here
Michael Rowe

SATURDAY, SEPTEMBER 13, by complete happenstance Justin Trudeau, the closest thing Canada has to a political celebrity, thanks in equal parts to his parentage and his handsomeness, came upon wedding group photograph at the Hilton hotel in Markham, Ontario. Famous politician that he is, he was asked by the photographer and by the bridal party if he wouldn't mind posing with them for a few shots. In one picture, he is kissing the bride on the cheek.

When the innocuous photos came to light, Sun News performer Ezra Levant saw raw meat for his viewers and pounced. The United States has Fox News, which is not only the most-watched television network in the nation, but a dependable source of manufactured scandal and outrage. In Canada, well, we have Ezra Levant on the Sun News Network, not usually as bloviating as your O'Reillys or Becks, but still not necessarily a fan of nuance. He hinted darkly at what he claimed was the Liberal leader's smug sense of entitlement ("The idea of the nobleman of the estate, riding through like in medieval times to deflower whatever maidens he wanted, that's still there in Trudeau," Levant gushed) and then took aim at both Trudeau's father, the late Prime Minister Pierre Elliot Trudeau, and the Liberal leader's 66-year old mother, employing the sort of sexual slurs usually reserved for use among teenage boys on a city bus.

In short order, Levant (who refers to himself on his website without irony as "Canada's foremost freedom fighter") ended up getting exactly what he wanted: many Canadians were outraged.

Though Levant's handful of devotees were made angry for the reasons he intended, mostly it was typical liberal Canadian outrage of the *Aren't we better than this?!* variety, and it only lasted about a week.

The tackiness of it all cut a bit too close to the bone for those of us who like to think Canadian media should be above the US cable news outrage-mongering sewage pumped out by Fox News and its ilk, who were just then beginning to work the US into the latest iteration of its patented add-a-bead paranoia and outrage—this time over how Ebola was basically President Obama's fault.

In the immediate aftermath, Trudeau announced that he was banning Sun News journalists from his press conferences until Sun News apologized for Levant's creepy five minute meltdown. They did.

For his part, Levant's own comments were, more or less, "No comment." He'd apparently accomplished exactly what he set out to accomplish, and had done so with a trollish *épater le bourgeois* score-settling instinct that would be familiar to any former high school nerd who hasn't gotten the taste of all the swirlies he received at the hands of the jocks out of his mouth.

In short, he'd hit his target: he'd outraged, he'd offended, he'd click-baited and he'd attracted some media coverage for his Sun TV cable show, then scampered off to giggle behind his fingers and enjoy the fallout.

Even though I knew Levant's outrage was calculated and transparent, I nonetheless found myself irresistibly drawn into heated online discussions with a handful of Levant's followers.

Maybe *discussion* is an overly generous term. It didn't occur to me at the time that in doing so I had become part of Levant's self-generating outrage machine. It was just something that I—that we—needed to do: someone was wrong on the Internet, and we were right.

By the time this is published, very few people will remember the Levant vs. Trudeau dustup without a prompt or two. Hell, at the time of this writing it's nearly forgotten. But that's exactly the point: we read a headline, an article, a tweet, are filled with righteous indignation, and blast our opinion into the ether. We feel momentarily satisfied, then check back to see if our comment has inspired any attaboys from our fellows or, perhaps, an outraged response of its own. And so the cycle continues.

For better or for worse, in one way or another these daily draughts of outrage, in wildly varying dosages, are now a part of the culture. Since we ourselves are obligatorily part of the culture, outrage is now part of us. We don't question it, we don't stop to think about why we're part of it, or how we might escape it, let alone any of the reasons why perhaps we should.

As is the case for most of us, my laptop (and increasingly, the screen of my phone) is as much my window to the outside world as any window in my house. Of late, between the ISIS massacres, Ebola, global warming, the erosion of women's reproductive rights in the United States, generic racism, animal cruelty, the pushback against LGBT equality, the increasing visibility of police brutality and the taken-for granted reality of a near-permanent state of war, I've absorbed more bad news via my homepage before I've finished my coffee than my parents' generation ever did in a week of newspaper reading and eleven o'clock news-watching.

Unlike my younger colleagues who have never known a pre-Internet world, I have a conscious memory of not starting my day with bad news, which usually results in irritation, anger, or anger's most bellicose cousin, outrage.

That's before I even check my Facebook and Twitter pages, where most of these stories have already been distilled and disseminated, sometimes with astute, intelligent contextualization and sometimes not, by friends, colleagues and strangers. With the engine running, I usually click "share" and join the outrage machine myself, passively, or with humour, or with reflexive, smug superiority, or with anger, but always with a sense of mission.

Like my response to the news that D-list has-been actor Kirk Cameron was campaigning to reclaim Halloween for the Lord: "Jesus wants Kirk Cameron to get a fucking life and stop embarrassing Him at parties."

Thus, the modern day begins. Both sides forcefully asserting the correctness of their point of view in whatever comment section the story ran; every participant shocked that someone could even entertain the position opposing their own. *Didn't they read the same news story as me? Haven't they googled what I've googled?*

In fact, no, they probably haven't.

While the Internet has given voice to anyone with a keyboard, it's also become a filter—a means of only hearing the voices we think we want to hear. So much of what we see and read is based on mysterious algorithms, sifting through our search history, our friends, our allegiances, that the news we consume often comes as tailored to our tastes as a drive-through hamburger and, most often, is just as nutritious.

Biologically speaking, the spectrum of emotions comprising anger and outrage are governed and stimulated in part by the amygdala, a cluster of almond-shaped nuclei located in the temporal lobes of the brain, the same nuclei that stimulates the fight-or-flight reaction to danger. One of the fundamental triggers of anger is fear. Even on the Internet.

Fear, in this context, is not limited to fear for one's own well-being or the well-being of loved ones. It also encompasses fear of personal humiliation, fear of the sanctity of one's own personal boundaries being breached to one's own self-esteem, even fear of a disruption of the acceptable moral social order as one experiences it, including, maybe especially, through abuses of power by those with power to abuse.

Some years back, I covered the true crime story of a 17-month-old baby who was beaten to death by his mother's live-in boyfriend because the man perceived the child had been acting "too feminine."

To my mind, the murderer was not the only monster in the story—or, at least, he wasn't the part of the story that instilled the most fear in me. The other monster was the insane societally supported logic that informed the man's lethal prejudices. Over the years, I've covered numerous stories about the abuse of power, but that one haunts me even today.

Interestingly, it's rarely the explicit villain of a story who sparks outrage—it's what those villains represent to the ones reading it. After Elliot Rodger went on his rampage last summer, killing six people and injuring 13 as a punishment for not getting laid, despite being a "nice guy," thus becoming the latest mass shooter to steal the media's spotlight, outrage wasn't directed at him—that he was a monster was a given, something everyone could agree on. What scared the commentariat more was the context. And while Matt Walsh, the popular right-wing religious blogger, and any given feminist *Jezebel* writer, might settle on different flavours of outrage—one decrying the obvious misogyny at work, the other the attention other writers seemed to be giving a murderer—fear was still at the heart of their vitriol. The one inevitable commonality is the anger that comes with an inexorable awareness that the world is not as we feel it should be.

In writing the story of that murdered baby, in sharing it, I was able offer it up for judgment, to extend an implicit invitation to readers to share my horror.

That, in a nutshell, is the engine that drives outrage culture, which in turn, drives the Internet in a vicious feedback loop. It makes sense that, through the web, we see more of the world, and thus have so many more opportunities to have reality crash into our expectations. In the positive sense, it can lead to a drive for social, political, or moral change. Or it can lead to a generalized, daily, seething cynicism that can be debilitating, not only for those experiencing it, but also for the people around them.

But if fear, and the resulting outrage, is unpleasant, why are we drawn to sharing bad news on social media? And more upsetting, why do we have the apparent in inability to distinguish between "legitimate" sources of outrage—at random, the Ferguson riots, for instance, or the murder of journalists in Syria or this past summer's Israel vs. Gaza conflict, all of which legitimately correlate to the very real condition of the world—as opposed to the various personal carryings-on and foibles of celebrities, or how "privileged" Gwyneth Paltrow is or how trashy the Kardashian sisters are, or the apparently devastating ethical implications of President Obama wearing a tan suit for a White House briefing? Or, for that matter, Ezra Levant calling Pierre Elliott Trudeau a "slut" on television? Because there is a difference. There has to be.

It turns out it's more about identity than morality.

"Outrage allows people to show their opinions. To express their identity. Even if everyone is against something, sharing that outrage allows us to come together and make it clear that our side or viewpoint is the right way to see things," says Jonah Berger, *New York Times* bestselling author of *Contagious: Why Things Catch On.* "These emotions fire us up and drive us to take action."

But that action is so often stunted, forgettable. Remember

KONY2012? #Bringbackourgirls? Any number of outrageous celebrity-backed causes that fell out of news cycles after a week, or month?

We've moved beyond our fundamental, reflexive human impulse to be naturally outraged and are now actively seeking outrage out and consuming it like any other commercial product. We're addicted to it.

And that addiction is made more powerful because we've attached a universal moral value to outrage for its own sake, whatever its actual cause or merits, as if all indignation was righteous. Critical thinking, in these cases, is often optional.

We're making it worse, even as we try to make it better. Look, for instance, at the rise of "trigger warnings." For those not in the know, a trigger warning is the grown-up equivalent to a parental advisory label; whatever proceeds might disturb the person consuming it or trigger a traumatic memory, often of violence or sexual assault, but also racism, homophobia or a plethora of other less easily quantifiable potential "emotional aggressions."

Trigger warnings make perfect sense in, say, feminist, African-American or LGBT primary spaces and blogs. But now, university professors have been asked to post them for required reading and lectures. The problem with trigger warnings in general use is that they colour the experience, pushing the consumer/reader toward outrage. If one is told there will be offensive content, one can't help look for it, ignoring context and intention. They oil up the outrage machinery, even while trying to mitigate negative reactions.

The problem with outrage as a means of social change, whether you're looking to oust a president you believe is "not a real American" (#Benghazi) or protect the rights of female video-game designers to not receive rape threats (#gamergate), is that, as both consumers and purveyors of outrage, both professional and amateur commentators are as likely to swarm for personal reasons as they are for those of the objective, popular good. Because it's about identity, outrage and hypocrisy tend to go hand in hand. We see great injustices, and what do we do? We troll other online trolls, instead of actually engaging in real work. "It's entertainment disguised as activism," says LA filmmaker Andrea James, who has written extensively on Internet outrage culture. "It makes them feel important and superior, but it rarely does much to address the underlying causes of iniquity. Outrage culture is the bastard child of Internet culture and consumer culture. It exists because a wide swath of people wants to feel like they're making a difference with the least amount of effort."

My friend's father has a saying. He doesn't know where his father got it, but he doesn't think he made it up: "Many a man prides himself on his virtue, when it is merely a lack of opportunity."

That saying comes to mind when I consider how comparable outrage might have been experienced by generations past. If there was less outrage then, it was because previous generations didn't have the means to express that outrage as openly and universally as the current generation does. It was judiciously considered and its merit weighed. Our parents might have written a letter to the editor, placed it in an envelope, licked the stamp, dropped it in a mailbox, and then sat back to see if it would be published. And, even then, that would be the end of it. The paradigm shift that birthed outrage culture wasn't just the immediacy with which we can register our horror, it was that we can—and are encouraged—to comment on the comments on the comments. It's dialogue: engagement, it's called. And it's as flammable in its way as an accidentally-dropped cigarette butt in the California forest in wildfire season.

While we are without a doubt better informed than our parents' generation ever could have dreamed of being, the nagging question is, what do we do with all that information? What's the purpose of having it? And at what point does all the bad news—and the outrage it engenders, coupled with our inability to effectively address it— simply become emotionally toxic, the spiritual equivalent of lactic acid buildup? Is there any point to being outraged any more?

For better or for worse, in addition to the stories I tell for a living, I maintain a daily running dialogue with thousands of strangers, usually but not always in an echo chamber of shared political and/ or moral perspectives. I'd like to think I bring a curatorial eye to the stories I share and comment on during my morning cull of the day's news, but I'm nonetheless feeding the fire of the outrage machine by doing so.

So, the question becomes, *why? Why do it? What's it about?* The answer is, *I don't know why.*

At its most redemptive level, the level I personally value, social media outrage is an effective tool for shining a light on injustice, and shaming that invisible monster in hopes that, at some point, the scrutiny and resulting shame becomes unbearable to the perpetrator. But Joseph Kony didn't particularly care what the Internet said about him. Neither does Ezra Levant. They continue to do what they do, supported by those who supported them before, and unimpeded by the outpouring of likes and hashtags and vitriolic online comments.

At its least redemptive level outrage is the insensate gibbering of emotionally ravenous, outraged strangers who are desperate— desperate—to feel something, anything, to connect, to not feel alone. The irony of feeling alone in a vortex of billions of virtual voices all shouting at once is nothing if not the quintessential paradox of the modern media age.

In the same way that you won't likely ever get Ebola, or effect political outcomes in any other way than by voting, the pernicious lure of outrage culture as is that it provides a temporary emotional fix disguised as action and participation. The long term net effect is not more immersion in the business of life, but potentially less, because after a while the realest window isn't the one to the actual world outside, it's the one that opens when you log on. Sorting through the outrage to separate the noise from what's real is the key.

The ability to maintain perspective, one of the oldest and most valuable lessons we learn in life, could be the one most quickly lost when we suddenly realize we're angry all the time, but can't for the life of us remember why.

Living Susan Sontag's Illness as Metaphor
Kenneth Sherman

THE FIRST BOOK I read on the subject of sickness was Susan Sontag's *Illness as Metaphor*. At the time, I was a healthy twenty-eight-year-old, and the terrain described in her book a distant land. Thirty-one years later, I was diagnosed with cancer and in an instant I belonged to Sontag's "kingdom of the sick." Major illness threw me into a disorienting emotional upheaval, and I experienced first-hand the bizarre and often morbid ways that one thinks about disease. To cope with my dread and foreboding, I read and reread a number of illness texts, including Sontag's insightful essay.

Given her own disturbing cancer experience, Sontag's restraint and objectivity toward her subject are remarkable. She gives not the slightest hint of the panic she must have felt when at age forty-two she was diagnosed with an advanced stage of breast cancer. Her goal in writing such an analytical book was utilitarian. As she explained ten years after *Illness as Metaphor* was published: "I didn't think it would be useful—and I wanted to be useful—to tell yet one more story in the first person of how someone learned that he or she had cancer, wept, struggled, was comforted, suffered, took courage…though mine was also that story."

Turning her penetrating gaze on illness imagery in literature and film, Sontag exposes some unpleasant and previously unacknowledged truths. She tells us that our views on illness are imbued with shame, fear, and self-vilification.

We disparage the seriously sick. Worse, the sick disparage themselves. Sontag intended her study as an antidote to the poisonous perceptions we hold about disease because it is those perceptions, she believed, that "deform the experience of having cancer." She hoped that her sober analysis might rid the patient of fearful metaphors (for instance, the sci-fi scenario in which the patient imagines him- or herself invaded by "mutant" or "alien" cells) and the awful self-negation that a dire diagnosis often triggers. Once liberated from those metaphoric trappings and critical pitfalls, the patient would make the best choices for treatment.

While I admire Sontag's attempt to strip cancer of its harmful associations, and while I agree with her that it is more helpful to think of illness as a biological mishap rather than the result of a personality defect, I found myself questioning her idea that "the most truthful way of regarding illness—and the healthiest way of being ill—is one most purified of, most resistant to, metaphoric thinking." In the grip of my cancer experience—an experience that forces the imagination to work overtime—I wondered if that was possible, or even wise.

Allow me to make clear the reality I was confronting and to illustrate the sort of thinking that is typical of the cancer patient. During a routine physical exam, my family doctor discovered a mass in my abdomen; an ultrasound showed that I had a very large tumour (fifteen centimetres) on my left kidney. The tumour was likely malignant and would have to be excised. The shock and disbelief that a diagnosis such as this engenders is great, and even greater if you are asymptomatic. You walk into a doctor's office feeling healthy, pain-free, and out of the blue you discover that you are facing a potentially terminal illness. I remember thinking, after the initial shock wore off, that some silent and subtle enemy had snuck up on me without rustling a single leaf. As you can see from the previous sentence, once you hear the news of your illness, the metaphoric thinking begins. It rarely lets up.

In my case, the size of the tumour was impressive, to say the least. My cancerous growth overshadowed my kidney (twelve centimetres), and I began to regard it as my kidney's nefarious double, my Bizarro World kidney, if you will, going back to my boyhood *Superman* comics. I began to consider my body, which I had exercised regularly and cared for, and which had served me well for so many years, a traitor. Unable to tell normal healthy cells from those that carry death, it had allowed this mass to grow unchecked—for at least ten years, according to my oncologist. I chastised my body for sleeping at the wheel, for being dumb and inarticulate. I knew from the little I had read about cancer that my own inner workings had produced these malignant cells and that the cells had disguised themselves in such a way as to be indistinguishable from healthy cells. They were hostile elements that I myself, astonishingly, created, and I had a grudging admiration for their ingenuity, their sly deceptiveness.

I found it impossible to avoid thinking about my disease in metaphors, just as I found it impossible, at first, to avoid self-blame. I worried that I grew this tumour because I hadn't eaten properly or had drunk water that was unfiltered. Perhaps my cancer was the result of those asbestos tiles I'd removed from the basement ceiling of our house soon after we'd moved in. Maybe it was the result of keeping my feelings bottled up, of leading a life of quiet desperation.

You can really work yourself over once you discover you have a serious illness. For the most part, I was able to limit self-blame by reminding myself that science has only begun to unlock the biochemical links to cancer, and that at present there seems to be a randomness to those who are stricken with most forms of the disease. But I couldn't stop the flow of imagery, and my intuition suggested that it would be unhealthy to repress the figurative reimagining of my illness. I knew from my years of reading and composing poetry that image-making is a vital dialogue with the self.

Giving my imagination free rein, I discovered allies in the books I was reading. Shortly after he was diagnosed with advanced prostate cancer, Anatole Broyard, the one-time literary critic for the *New York Times*, wrote, "the sick man sees everything as metaphor." He viewed this as a plus. In his book *Intoxicated by My Illness*, Broyard criticized Sontag for "being too hard on metaphor." As he says, "metaphors may be as necessary to illness as they are to literature. … At the very least, they are a relief from medical terminology… only metaphor can express the bafflement, the panic combined with beatitude, of the threatened person." Broyard had written his book as he was dying. Illness books that are written while the angel of death hovers are exceptionally rich in metaphor, I noted. Novelist Harold Brodkey, dying of AIDS, described himself as "a small bird nervous in the shadow, a bag of tainted blood." It's as if figurative language were acting as a type of palliative.

John Keats praised "the truth of the imagination," and it may be that such truth originates in our very cells. Reading Dr. Siddhartha Mukherjee's *The Emperor of All Maladies: A Biography of Cancer*, I was startled to realize that envisioning my cancer as an ill-intentioned double, a malignant, disguised version of me, is in keeping with recent scientific assessments. For Mukherjee, a devoted oncologist, cancer is "a parallel species…more adapted to survival than we are." He deems it "our desperate, malevolent, contemporary doppelganger." His amazement rests on one undeniable fact: "Cancer cells can grow faster, adapt better. They are more perfect versions of ourselves." Such figurative language captures the awe, the astonishment of having cancer; I prefer it to the cold, clinical terminology of the CT scan report I was handed with my diagnosis.

Though I had the good fortune to survive my disease, I was given an inordinately long time to think about my tumour. Due to those well-publicized backlogs in our health-care system, I was forced to wait an unconscionable two and a half months before a surgeon would remove my cancerous growth. I often envisioned my tumour as a fetus getting larger and larger, myself pregnant with my approaching death. My doctors speculated that the cancer had metastasized, and I saw the malignant cells coursing through my blood as spy ships sent out from the Central Tumour, looking for other organs to invade. I should note that none of these imaginings are unique or out of the ordinary. Once you read a number of illness memoirs, you realize that being sick can render your imagination quotidian; it's a levelling experience that binds you to suffering humanity. (Of course, if you're a talented writer, à la Brodkey, you can convey your experience in language that is fresh and startling.) I should also note, contra Sontag, that my metaphoric thinking didn't deter me from seeking the best possible doctors and treatment. Rather, the terror of my imaginings spurred me to action.

Shortly after my surgeries, I read Sontag's newly published journals, which had been edited by her son, David Rieff; I also read the harrowing memoir (*Swimming in a Sea of Death*) that Rieff had written about his mother's third, and final, battle with cancer. What I hadn't known when I read Sontag's *Illness as Metaphor* was that it had been written, in Rieff's words, "long after her treatments had ended and all seemed to be well," when she could look back on her frightening experience with some degree of equanimity. In the mid-1970s, Sontag had been diagnosed with stage IV metastatic breast cancer (the disease had spread to seventeen of her lymph nodes) and doctors at New York's Sloan Kettering Cancer Center held out little hope. Driven by a strong will to survive, Sontag did her own research and found a doctor in Paris who was willing to administer a more aggressive, experimental chemotherapy regime; this likely saved her life. But Rieff discloses that when his mother was first diagnosed, she engaged in the same sort of punishing emotions and metaphoric thinking that she later warned others against. For instance, upon learning of her illness, she played the self-blame game. As an intellectual, she had flirted with the highly suspect Reichian theory, which held that blocked desires—especially sexual desires—cause cancer. "I'm responsible for my cancer," she wrote in one of her journals. "I lived as a coward, repressing my desire, my rage." And when she began chemotherapy, she indulged in extreme forms of metaphoric thinking: "I feel like the Vietnam War," she wrote. "My body is invasive, colonizing. They're using chemical weapons on me." Given her inquisitive and polemical nature, at some point after her illness Sontag began to question what she had thought and felt about having cancer. The skeptical brilliance of *Illness as Metaphor* speaks of one who's come through and wishes to dispel the defeatist, punitive notions of cancer so that those who follow may be less burdened. A noble project. But Rieff argues, convincingly, that it was not Sontag's analytical powers so much as her obstinate attachment to living (what he calls "her steely resolve") that guided her choice of aggressive therapies and prolonged her life.

The significant time that Sontag waited to write her classic book allowed her to distance herself from an experience she found excruciatingly painful. It permitted her to think critically about our social and historical attitudes toward cancer. But her distancing also cut her off from the immediacy of the sickness experience and led her to limit our imaginings, unaware that our metaphors are the deepest expressions we have, and that by voicing them we tap a source of inner strength.

Fault Lines
Antanas Sileika

Not only is Canada a mosaic, but many Canadians are mosaics within themselves. Given this complexity of identity, what does it mean to remember and to memorialize? Why do we commemorate some events and not others? What events should be memorialized?

At a Canadian embassy office reception in Vilnius some years ago while on a research trip, I was chatting with the chargé d'affaires while waiting to meet my son, who was on leave in the middle of deployment with the Van Doos Canadian infantry regiment in Afghanistan. Now there was an example of a mosaic: a Lithuanian heritage Canadian deployed in the French language in a foreign county.

The chargé d'affaires was interested in my son, but he was also interested in me. He wanted to know what a Canadian like me was researching in Lithuania. I told him I was working on a novel about the anti-Soviet postwar resistance in Lithuania.

He didn't exactly bristle, but I noted a subtle change in his tone, a sense of disappointment, as if I should have chosen another story of suffering in Lithuania, perhaps the Holocaust, which had been particularly brutal in that country. At the time, there was intense discussion going on about Eastern Europe's

151

failure to deal with its Holocaust past.

It was hard to tell precisely what the problem was because we were speaking polite code. Finally, the chargé suggested that unlike Canada, there was altogether too much history in Lithuania and the rest of Europe.

And now it seems that there is too much history in Canada too. Conflicting memories clash in the controversy surrounding the plan to build the Victims of Communism Memorial in Ottawa.

This memorial has been attacked vigorously in many places, among them by *The Globe and Mail* journalist Roy MacGregor. He and other commentators have derided the project on several grounds: as ugly, as misplaced in a location, as an example of government's currying favour with particular groups of ethnic voters, and finally as an unnecessary and even lamentable example of a memorial that has nothing to do with Canada's history.

I catch a whiff of disingenuity in all this opposition. I concede the site on prime Ottawa real estate may be a mistake. The design may be bad. But why should an officially sanctioned monument to the victims of communism offend so many? Here are a few hypotheses.

Many progressives hate anything the Harper government does. Because his rule is deemed deplorable, everything he turns his hand to must be deplorable. Indeed, when Harper upbraided Vladimir Putin before reluctantly shaking hands with him, many of my Facebook friends, a progressive literary lot if ever there was one, vilified Harper, claiming he was just playing up to ethnic voters. Critics further left who are apologists for Russia even claimed Putin was forced into defensive actions against the hegemonic West. When I attempted to defend Harper's upbraiding of Putin by writing that sometimes people you do not like do the right thing, I took a firestorm of derision.

As an aside here, since I have a rather strong connection with events going on in Eastern Europe, I was called by a radio show in Lithuania and asked how it was possible that Harper had the courage to say to Putin what other western leaders did not. After all, millions of Poles, Balts, and Ukrainians breathed sighs of relief at Harper's words, and still the harpies in Canada sneered. Interestingly, at least one Lithuanian columnist speculated that Harper, as the ruler of a middle nation, was designated spokesman for the western point of view, permitting Canada to say what larger powers could not.

To recap, some of the opposition to the memorial lies in ad hominem attacks against Harper. The Harper government supports the memorial to the victims of communism. Ergo the memorial must be bad.

Second, during the Cold War, communism was the enemy of the old postwar right of America and Canada. At the time, my leftish generation and those older than me preferred to focus on issues such as apartheid in South Africa, the plight of grape pickers in California, and the revolution in Nicaragua. Back then anti-communist sentiments were uncool, to say the least. For many contemporary progressives, these sentiments continue to carry whiffs of fusty conservatism. Indeed, the preferred progressive narrative of the cold war seems to focus upon those who suffered under McCarthyism, when Hollywood screenwriters and others were losing their jobs rather than upon those who were in in slave camps or being executed by communist regimes.

Thus a lingering left bias sees the monument to the victims of communism as an extension of the old politics of the right. But progressives are a relatively small minority of Canada's population. Others have views on the proposed monument too.

For immigrants to this country, Canada is a kind of benign island for those who were lucky enough to survive the worldwide shipwrecks of politics and war and have washed up upon these safe and wealthy shores. Those who end up here, or their children, eventually reflect back on what happened, and they begin to memorialize. This is particularly true of East Europeans who believed they were betrayed by the west and abandoned to the tyranny of the Soviet Union. Since no one else seemed to know or care about what had happened there, Eastern Europeans had to do their commemorating for themselves.

It takes a long time for memory to assert itself and spur memorialization. It took decades for the well-known facts about the Holocaust to open the subject to vast coverage in the media and in new history books. Yet although we may believe we have heard much about the Holocaust, historian Timothy Snyder says we have only now begun to understand how woefully unknown so much of the Holocaust remains because most of it occurred not in Auschwitz, but further East in the killing fields in the Baltics, Belarus, and Ukraine.

Similarly, a quarter century after the fall of the Soviet Union and decades after the revelation of the horrors of Cambodia and the extent of deaths under Mao, the profundity of the outrage of communism has begun to sink in, and people have begun to memorialize. It takes time to assimilate the knowledge of tragedy and to respond to it. Sometimes it takes a very long time.

An example of this delay can be seen in the Canadian reaction to the destruction of native culture in Canada. It is only now that the Truth and Reconciliation Commission is revealing the full horror of the attempt at cultural annihilation. It is only now that the Supreme Court is beginning to recognize the full extent of native rights over vast tracts of Canadian land. We always knew that the land had been taken from the natives, but in some way we did not fully grasp what that meant. Truth has been revealed, but reconciliation is still a project that will take decades to understand, let alone implement.

So it has taken time to memorialize the victims of communism, but this particular commemoration raises other sorts of issues.

Some of the most moving memorials in the world are Holocaust memorials, and indeed, a Holocaust memorial is being built in Ottawa and neither the design nor the placement of it has caused any kind of controversy in the press, although the comments sections below newspaper articles echo some of objections raised by journalists against the victims of communism memorial.

The success in broadcasting the news of the Holocaust may have motivated others to publicize their own sufferings, such as the Ukrainian Holodomor and the murder of the Armenians in Turkey. The term "survivors," once applied solely to Holocaust survivors, has now entered the lexicon to cover survivors of cultural genocide, sexual abuse and other crimes. And so, controversially, has the term "genocide" which in initial negotiations over the genocide convention in 1947 was intended to include mass murders of non-ethnic or religious groups such as intelligentsias, until the definition was narrowed due to Soviet objections. The Soviets had to object because they would have been guilty of the charge of genocide in, for example, the attacks on kulaks. As well, had the Soviets not objected, their attempts to destroy local intelligentsias would have been called genocide too, such as the Soviet murder of Polish officers in the Katyn Forest.

And this brings us to another problem with a monument to the victims of communism, at least those who died in Europe. We like clear narratives, but history is sadly short of such stories. The Jews who survived the Holocaust in Eastern Europe did so mostly thanks to Soviet armies, which were the main actors in the defeat of Nazism and the only ones in the east. Those same Soviet armies went on to rape and pillage much of Eastern Europe and helped to install tyrannies throughout the region, as depicted so well in Anne Applebaum's justly celebrated account *Iron Curtain*.

So were the Soviets liberators or invaders? It depends on which victims you ask. Further, were the victims of communism sometimes those who did not help Jews, or, in some cases, those who actively participated in the Nazi-inspired atrocities? How are we to tease out those who suffered for their crimes versus those who suffered for no other reason than falling under the sway of a tyrannical regime?

This particular problem is acute in Eastern Europe, where there have been accusations that the attempt to remember the victims of communism is a ploy to disguise the actions of Nazi collaborators. Further aggravation in some circles came from the Prague declaration of 2008, which sought to memorialize the victims of Stalinism and Nazism. Some Holocaust interpreters have called this a form of moral equivalency and have stated that the two tyrannies must never be compared. But as has been noted by several commentators, if you say Nazism and communism should not be compared, you have already done so.

In short, the story of the victims of communism, at least in Europe, potentially collides with the Holocaust story. There is no easy way to avoid this collision.

Memorials and memory are often anathema to historians. The late Tony Judt said that memory cannot substitute for history. In his words, "official commemoration...does not enhance our appreciation and awareness of the past. It serves as a substitute, a surrogate. Instead of teaching history we walk children through museums and memorials."

But most people are bored by history. In my experience, Canadians know little history, but everyone seems to have an opinion about it: at worst, the past in the popular view was less enlightened than we are, a kind of horror show. As well, many Canadian writers, in particular younger ones, deplore historical fiction because it romanticizes the past. As implied in the title of

Milan Kundera's novel, *The Book of Laughter and Forgetting*, maybe we should forget in order to laugh, because otherwise, history is a terrible place.

If practically no one reads history after high school, what's left but memory and memorials?

I recently stood in the Dawn Gate of Vilnius, the last remaining portal in the medieval defensive walls of that city. Through that gate, German prisoners of war were marched to show them off to the war weary inhabitants. The city had been freed by the Soviets, but also by Polish Armia Krajowa soldiers who intended to seize the city for Poland. Rather than thank the Poles, after the liberation the Soviets and killed or deported those who did not escape. Before that, near the beginning of the war, thousands of Jews must have passed through those gates on the way to being butchered in the Ponary forest. Before that, local residents were marched through by the newly arrived Soviets to be shipped off to the gulag and almost certain death among the early Soviet deportees. And if we keep on going back, we find the remains of Napoleon's Grand Armée ran through those gates to be hunted and hacked to death by czarist soldiers.

If one small place has so many layers, is such a palimpsest of history, how are we to determine what needs to be remembered and what needs to be forgotten? To return to Milan Kundera in his novel *Life Is Elsewhere*, "How sweet it would be to forget history!"

Yet Kundera can also be quoted again to illustrate what we are about when we build memorials: "The novelist demolishes the house of his life and uses its bricks to construct another house: that of his novel."

Novelists are not the only ones involved in this act. Societies demolish the house of history and use its bricks to construct another house: that of memory as expressed in memorials.

While we know that memory is selective, it remains a powerful force in shaping us as individuals and in determining what we do as societies.

Canada has over a million citizens of Polish heritage, and even more Ukrainians, a scattering of Balts and many tens of thousands of Vietnamese. For many of them, memories of sufferings under communism remain vivid, whether the suffering happened to them or their parents. Why should we deny their suffering and their right to remember it?

If there are other events which need to be memorialized, let those who want to do so go ahead and lobby the government to do so officially. We can object to design, we can object to placement, and we can object to the use of taxpayers' dollars. But to dismiss the need to remember and memorialize is to trivialize the suffering of others.

As to the detractors who say we should only remember events in which Canada played a role, those millions of immigrants and their children are indeed Canadians. Their memories are the memories of this country too. As with the memory of what happened and is happening to native people, we are coming late to an understanding of the past, however imperfect that understanding may be. We should now make up for lost time.

Landowner Rights
Fred Stenson

ALBERTA SCENARIO. A family pays for its city mortgage and decides to move to an acreage. They buy a place and settle into country living. An oil company fracks near their home. Soon after, they notice their water does not taste right.

Alberta families who believe they have been harmed by industrial activity usually assume they have property rights that are being violated. Many believe the government will help them, at least in gaining compensation. The truth is that Canada's Constitution and the Canadian Charter of Rights and Freedoms are silent on property rights.

As Canadians, we think we have property rights because it is a natural thing to assume in a democratic nation. Property ownership is a gauge of our security and a storehouse for our savings. Professors Eran Kaplinsky and David Percy, authors of the Alberta Land Institute's *A Guide to Property Rights in Alberta*, describe assumptions we make about the property we own: that we will be able to use and enjoy it, develop it as we desire, exclude others from it and sell it to whomever we please. But in Canada the ultimate right over property belongs to the Crown. The government can do with our property more or less as it pleases.

Many Canadian federal and provincial statutes affirm the

Crown's right to take or use property for the public good. If land is needed for an airport, government can expropriate. When the Crown leases mineral rights—to an oil company, for example—the usual practice is for a company landman to negotiate access with the surface rights owner. Payment is offered but refusal to allow access isn't an option. If the owner will not play, the government can grant the oil company a right of access. The same goes for plants, pipelines and transmission lines.

On some level, most of us understand expropriation for the public good. When a city needs infrastructure, it often has no choice but to expropriate someone's property. Roads and utilities must go somewhere. Alberta, with a relatively small population compared to its land area, depends on natural resources for public funds. In return for royalties, industry gets access.

Some of us will be unlucky enough to be in the way of infrastructure or industrial projects and will be called on to sacrifice. The alternative—and the US system with constitutional property rights defines that alternative—is for people to be allowed to refuse. Even in the US, however, the government has a power of "eminent domain" that can overrule property rights.

Government also needs Crown power over property to carry out policy. A recent example was emergency action to save the sage grouse from being wiped out in Canada. To protect sage grouse, the provincial government in 2013 took back private grazing rights on the birds' breeding grounds. If we think expropriation is "government against the little guy in support of corporations," many would feel it is unfair. If it means protecting an endangered species, more of us are comfortable with it.

The truth is that a system like Alberta's only functions smoothly if the government's and citizens' definitions of "public good" are the same. A lack of common understanding leads to confrontation. Many Alberta landowners feel the province's regulatory bodies reflexively choose industry over property owners and therefore public trust has eroded. To protect the enjoyment of their property, their health, and their property value, owners feel forced to do battle with their own government.

In recent years one Alberta landowner's struggle with an oil company and the Alberta government stands out above the rest, partly because of the incredibly stubborn determination of the complainant. Jessica Ernst's failure to get satisfaction for the pollution of her water supply after fracking has grown into a seven-year lawsuit. To understand Ernst's situation—and the many similar to hers—we need to understand first how Alberta property rights came to be so lopsidedly pro-industry.

It starts with mineral rights. At a glance, the biggest difference between land ownership in the US and Canada is that most American landowners own surface and mineral rights together (called freehold), while most Canadians own surface rights only. The simplest answer as to why this is so is that Crown ownership is a British tradition that Canada followed when it became a nation. The US achieved nationhood by violent rebellion against British rule. Hence, Americans own freehold rights and Canadians do not.

Some privately owned mineral rights do exist in Canada, usually where ownership predates nationhood (Ontario, Quebec, the Maritimes). By the time Alberta became a province (1905), homesteaders were limited to owning surface rights. In Alberta today, the province owns 81 per cent of mineral rights and the federal government owns 9 per cent. The remaining 10 per cent of mineral rights in private hands is the result of old deals such as freehold property given to the Canadian Pacific Railway as part of the company's original agreement with Canada. Those mineral rights are now owned by Encana Corporation.

In Alberta's first four decades as a province, mineral rights were not avidly sought after. Except for gas at Medicine Hat and oil at Turner Valley, Alberta was considered barren of petroleum. Imperial Oil punched many dry holes to prove that—but then came Leduc. Imperial's 1947 oil strike just south of Edmonton ushered in a new concept of Albertan resource wealth. The key that unlocked Leduc unlocked many reservoirs. After 1947, Alberta mineral rights were golden.

Oil dragged Alberta out of a post-war economic abyss. The Social Credit government found itself at the helm of a fast-growing province with money piling up in its coffers. It is not so surprising that Alberta's government felt beholden to oil companies for its prosperity.

In the 1950s and 1960s, oil ruled Alberta. When a company wanted to drill, build or run a pipeline, farmers were pushed aside. That treatment could be rough. When a 1960s sour gas plant south of Pincher Creek malfunctioned (the gas literally eating the high-grade steel meant to contain it), families downwind were regularly dosed with poisonous hydrogen sulphide. Pigs died at such a rate that the farmers gave up on pork production. Families with sick children moved away. When an Alberta government health study found no serious health risks, local families started a lawsuit that was settled twelve years later.

This out-of-court settlement was important in that farmers had pushed a big oil company to pay. Otherwise the victory was moral only. Government did not admit its health study was flawed. Industry did not admit it had killed or sickened anyone or anything.

In these ways, the compact between oil and government was forged. Politically, the only upheaval came in 1971 when Peter Lougheed's Progressive Conservatives defeated Social Credit and brought in tougher oil and gas regulations. The PCs have run

Alberta ever since. Those who say nothing has changed point to oil. Alberta remains a one-trick, one-resource pony.

All this may be masking a contradictory-sounding truth: that Alberta has changed too much not to change. In the three generations since Leduc, Alberta's population has grown from 800,000 to over four million. Calgary and Edmonton grew past the million mark, as rural domination turned to urban domination. While many Albertans vote PC and work for oil companies, Albertans generally are not the same people who were buoyed by the 1950s oil-tide. We are less grateful. After having "barrelled" through its conventional oil supply, with little in the bank to show for it, Alberta's government shifted focus to higher-cost, environmentally destructive bitumen. In recent years, the oil sands has not balanced Alberta's books either, because of a sweet royalty deal Ralph Klein gave oil sands developers in the 1990s. While Norway used North Sea oil royalties to save $829-billion (about a million Norwegian kroner per citizen), Alberta has saved $17.4-billion from its entire conventional oil resource. Having duped itself in the oil sands, the province has charged into its third petroleum frontier: hydraulic fracturing. When Albertans hear it said that oil companies love doing business in low-tax Alberta, it turns us cynical. The public good has long since become the industry good.

The oil sands has been an environmental and public relations disaster for Alberta, but fracking may wind up being the petroleum frontier that shakes Alberta hard enough to alter its fundamentals. Fracking is farm-by-farm, acreage-by-acreage property invasion. Much of it is done in the acreage belt around cities and towns. This time, industry is not just battling farmers or "radical environmentalists"; it is in conflict with people who often purchased rural property with proceeds from careers in the oil industry—the kind of middle class Albertans who put the PCs in office. Real estate studies show that fracking on or near your land can reduce sale value by as much as 25 per cent. Income studies show that most Canadians hold their retirement savings in real estate. Combine these and you have an attack on middle-class worth, on Albertans' hopes for their future.

Jessica Ernst moved to her acreage at Rosebud in 1998. She is a biologist who owns an environmental services company. Among her clients in the 1980s was PanCanadian (the company that merged with AEC to form Encana in 2002).

In 2003 Encana expanded a coalbed methane development in southern Alberta. An Encana brochure described the process as pumping nitrogen into coal seams to separate "cleats" in the coal and produce channels through which methane can flow. Some of those wells were drilled at Rosebud, and after shallow fracking took place near her home, Jessica Ernst's water changed suddenly. Her taps whistled; she could light the water on fire. Her dogs refused to drink it. Her skin burned when she showered. None of these problems had existed before.

Ernst called Encana about the water problem and was, she says, "dismissed within minutes." She was also troubled by incredible compressor noise during fracks, well above legal limits, and because of this separate issue, Encana offered to move her. When an *Edmonton Journal* article appeared about her water problem, Encana cancelled the relocation offer.

Ernst pursued her water problem with the Energy and Utilities Board. The EUB told a reporter that the regulator had tested Ernst's water and found no methane. This EUB person also told the reporter that Jessica was making up her story to get attention. Ernst says this conversation between EUB and a reporter happened before any government investigation of her water had taken place.

Something very similar happened when she took the issue to

Alberta Environment. Ernst says that before Environment did any testing of her water, someone from that department told a reporter that her water problem was bacterial.

In 2005 the EUB cut off communication with Ernst, denying her access to their investigation and complaints process. The stated reason was a mention of the "Wiebo way" in an Ernst email. (Alberta farmer Wiebo Ludwig was convicted in 2000 of sabotaging oil and gas wells.) Ernst says that, in her email, she made it clear she was quoting a neighbour. Nonetheless, EUB decided what she had written constituted a "criminal threat of violence" that they reported to the RCMP.

Ernst's lawyer at the time thought she should apologize to the chair of the regulator. Ernst refused. "Only in cycles of abuse do victims think they should apologize when they get beaten up," was her comment. Much later, in 2006, a lawyer for the EUB told Ernst that they had never considered her a threat. is suggested the purpose had been to silence her.

When Alberta Environment finally did investigate Jessica Ernst's water, she became convinced they were not doing so in good faith. In 2007 she resorted to the courts. Her $33-million suit was against Encana, ERCB and Alberta Environment for the contamination of her water and failures of regulation and investigation. (The EUB had become the ERCB in the interim.) She also contended that the decision by ERCB to ban her from their regulatory process denied her Charter right to free expression.

Ernst's life has been completely absorbed by this lawsuit and by communicating with people and media on fracking and water contamination. Efforts to undermine her credibility have been ongoing, including a whisper campaign about her sanity. When farmers asked oil company landmen about Ernst's problems with fracking, some said not to listen to her, that she was a crazy woman. A dirty business.

As Ernst's lawsuit proceeded, the Alberta Energy Regulator (formerly ERCB; formerly EUB) contended it "owed no duty of care" to protect anyone's groundwater in Alberta; also that an eco-terrorist's Charter rights could be violated by a regulator. (Although Ernst has never been charged by the RCMP, the word "terrorist" was applied to her in court documents led by the Alberta Energy Regulator in 2012.) Alberta Environment argued that words such as "hazardous," "pollutants" and "contamination" should be removed from Ernst's statement of claim. This department also wanted removed any suggestions that Ernst's experiences were related to those of others claiming water contamination from fracking.

The Alberta government stands solidly behind its fracking industry. In February 2013, when confronting an NDP contention that domestic water supplies were being contaminated by fracking, Premier Alison Redford described the claims as "completely false." Industry and government had also operated in tandem in the 1960s, when southern Alberta farmers tried to sue for air pollution. No animal deaths were admitted then; no water contamination from fracking is admitted now.

During the years of Ernst's lawsuit, Alberta passed legislation that further weakened the rights of landowners. Bill 19 gave Cabinet the power to assemble land without expropriating it, to make it available later for uses such as pipelines and highways (a status that would greatly depress property value). Bill 36 confirmed that decisions about the use of private land could be made by Cabinet. Bill 50 removed protections for people living in the path of proposed power lines by moving the decision of whether such lines were needed to Cabinet (no public hearing). Rather than responding to public concerns, the government was creating new ways to keep the public out of the discussion.

In September 2013, Alberta chief justice Neil Wittmann ruled on Ernst's right to sue. He found the Alberta Energy Regulator immune from legal claims. In his summation, however, he supported Ernst's objection to the way the energy regulator had used the email mention of "Wiebo" to restrict her speech. He said she had been denied her opportunity to "register her serious and well-founded concerns."

In response to the finding that the Alberta Energy Regulator was immune from her claims, Ernst felt she had no choice but to appeal. "Justice Wittmann has ruled that ERCB has a duty to protect the public, but not me. I *am* the public."

In 2014 government lawyers tried to strike Ernst's suit on grounds that it would lead to masses of litigation and cost the government "millions and billions." Though likely an exaggeration, it was true that more Albertans were coming forward with complaints about fracking—and were running into similar blockades from regulatory bodies. The Hawkwood ranching family from the Cochrane-Lochend area northwest of Calgary have been running a similar gauntlet to that of Jessica Ernst. They believe that flaring of solution gas at fracking sites has caused them health problems. When they approached AER, they were told go to Alberta Environment. Alberta Environment turned them away because they had 400 similar complaints from southern Alberta.

The Hawkwoods are part of a project called Alberta Voices (albertavoices.ca), which has filmed interviews with local landowners with industry-related concerns, a body of information available to the general public.

Any suggestion that Ernst's problems are non-existent, isolated or restricted to shallow fracking are contradicted by the number and geographical spread of similar complaints: Spirit River, Wetaskiwin, Cochrane, Ponoka, Didsbury—to name just a few Alberta sources.

The struggle by Alberta landowners to get fair treatment from oil companies and government has resulted in a proliferation of landowner groups. The issue is not always petroleum. Energy transmission lines too pose a threat to land value, not just where the line runs but everywhere within sight. Nearby owners suffer their losses without any hope of compensation. In Alberta the public purse pays for the lines and the power companies own them—a formula for over-building if there ever was one. Once again, the "public good" argument is tainted.

On November 10, 2014, Jessica Ernst was back in court before Justice Wittmann. The case had been underway since April 16, 2014. Now the judge was ready to rule—and Ernst came away with a victory.

While standing by his earlier decision that Alberta Energy Regulator was immune from prosecution, Wittmann ruled that Alberta Environment could be sued for failure to properly investigate: "I find that there is a reasonable prospect Ernst will succeed in establishing that Alberta owed her a *prima facie* duty of care." For the improper manner in which her claim had been attacked, Wittmann awarded Ernst triple her costs.

Ernst's response: "This is a big victory for water and for all Albertans. The decision means that landowners can stand up and hold governments and regulators to account." In another interview, she said, "There is still a lot of hell ahead. The government maintains that fracking is safe and that all methane contamination of water wells is natural. I think my lawsuit, which is built on corporate and regulatory data, will prove things differently." As for her belief that the ERCB denied her Charter rights, Ernst has applied to take that complaint to Canada's Supreme Court. The awarding of triple costs did not impress her, however, for it had cost her far more than the $9,000 awarded to protect her case from the attempts to have it thrown out.

Those who own property in Alberta are more accustomed to bad news than good. But the breakthrough in the Ernst case was one of three late-2014 "good news" land stories. In December the Alberta Electric System Operator ordered AltaLink to stop all activities on three electricity transmission projects that southern Alberta landowner groups had been fighting for some time. The justification for the lines—gathering wind power—will be re-evaluated.

A month before that, Alberta's new premier Jim Prentice (a property lawyer by background) repealed Bill 19, the odious land assembly law. In a November 17 speech from the throne, premier Prentice's government said it was signalling "the beginning of government's commitment to rebuild relationships with property owners in Alberta."

Many, like Jessica Ernst, will need to see it to believe it.

Six Ways She Might Have Died before She Reached Nineteen
Leona Theis

1. *In utero*

NOT EVERYONE GETS out alive. This one's mother had a miscarriage—one at least—years before. The girl would learn about it at the age of ten or thereabouts, when Grandma of the Despairing Outlook came to visit. Grandma swept the kitchen, and as she swept she mumbled lamentations: her daughter in such a marriage, *such* a marriage; even this floor, sharp with splinters, stubborn against the broom; a hard life, and this harsh wood the least of it. Grandma's mumbles stumbled back through years, to land on the outside staircase leading up to the first apartment of the marriage, a staircase the bride went down and up in all weathers, carrying babies, carrying groceries, carrying water pails up and the slop pail down. No wonder she'd ended up in hospital with the aftermath of a miscarriage.

But life improved, or changed at least, and by the time the final babe was curled inside the womb, the mother, along with the father and the one-year-old and the toddler and the daughter about to start school, had moved to a house with a street-level entrance. The lucky child scooched down the slick canal and slip-slopped out as a baby's meant to do. No staircase now, but still the mother carried babies, carried groceries, carried water pails in and the slop pail out, as did so many of her generation; as do so many women still. Life goes on. I know half a dozen women, myself included, who've experienced miscarriage through no fault of heavy lifting or ill-made marriage. It happens; causes vary. For the record, in this case Despairing Grandma might have got it right.

2. *Riding in cars with boys*

Drunken driving was typical Saturday night transpor-*tainment* in Prairie towns in the early seventies. A pair of cars would pull into the railway station parking lot, driver's door to driver's. The boys would crank their windows down, rev their engines—*What you got under there?*—and trade what they liked to call intelligence on the whereabouts of parties. There was Jimmy Dutch one night, telling them which road to look for, then which turnoff, then which stand of bush. Not yet *shundown* and already he was *shlurring*. "You'll shee my car when you get there. It'll be parked, uh, on its roof." What merriment. Jimmy drove a white ragtop, which gave his joke an extra torque, the image of that stretched, pale canvas dump-bump-thumping to a stop in gravel and wild grass.

Jimmy survived that night. The lucky girl survived a couple of years of nights like that, doing things her mother warned against. The usual number didn't.

3. *Riding in cars with her mother*

She was riding shotgun in the long, dark Mercury Meteor; her mother had the wheel. Dusk: neither day nor evening, but the soft sash between.

"Mom, you're going too fast."

Narrow highway, unshouldered; double solid lines up the middle like a zipper, closed.

Eyes ahead, her mom made no reply.

"*Mom?*"

Mouth cinched.

Her mother had fetched her from a friend's house: parked the Meteor, strode up the sidewalk to the front door, knocked rap-rap, ordered the girl to the car. Sped through town flicking gravel, shot onto the highway. Something had happened, who knew what. She'd been humiliated by something her husband had done or failed to do. He wasn't an awful man, but flawed, and the two of them a tragic match. Humiliations had gathered year by year. A cloud of them condensed against the cold window of that moment in the Meteor.

"What are you *do*ing?"

Her mother's voice a wire, taut: "I'm going," she said—and the wire began to vibrate—"to kill us both." So pitiful little was ever under this woman's control, but for those few moments she held sway over a steering wheel, an accelerator, and the choice of how to use them. By and by she made her choice, possibly the harder one: she eased up on the accelerator, found an approach, made an inexpert three-point turn, steered home in the early dark and took things up where she'd left off, for better and worse and to make her way. *Brava.*

4. Unsupervised swimming

A dock, a lake, a party-ready posse of teenagers on a hot afternoon. A car parked on the grass, doors open, music blaring, trunk a toothless gape. Something by The Doors? Was she fifteen? Escaped, for a time, from the hometown, the household, the boys who might rather she didn't tag along in their cars with the other girls anyhow. Summer vacation with cousin Shannon and family, and they'd busted loose for the afternoon, she and Shannon. The point of the shenanigans on the dock in the sunshine was to check out the contours of the opposite sex in bathing suits, to blush and touch and half-pretend you hadn't, to engineer what would happen and with whom, come the dark. Light my fire. She wore a blue bikini with splashy white flowers. The metal clasp at the nape of her neck would sometimes slip undone if she moved her shoulders in a certain way. More than once in the history of that bikini, the clasp had failed and the bra had fallen open upside-down, two fabric triangles hanging small and limp against her midriff, her undergrown breasts feeling the air. Roughhousing on the dock that day she was careful of her movements, more concerned with that clasp than with other dimensions of personal safety.

A boy caught her up. One of his boy-arms lifted her bare legs and the other circled her shoulders, and his sweaty boy-stomach pressed into her bare-skin side as he hefted her. Excitement squirmed low in her gut. He flung her away, away, into the drink and past her depth. Her cousin shouted, "She can't swim!" and that was true, not even a passable dog paddle. The girl in the splashy bikini panicked and thrashed and possibly thought it was over, all of it, the bright and the dark and the shouldn't-matter-but-it-does.

And then she surfaced, a-splutter and a-gasp. To her cousin's wonder and her own she kept her head above water, lungs hoovering, airways drawing tight in fear of water rushing in. She managed a lame-legged frog-kick back to the dock, put a hand to the nape of her neck to check the clasp, then let the boys haul her up, her bra plastered against her standup nipples. Her own dramatic surfacing that afternoon is what she remembers, rather than what happened after dark, or with whom.

I'm not what's called a natural. I never have developed the knack of swimming properly, not with my face in the water, emptying my lungs at the right moment and coming up for air between strokes. But if the necessary thing is to cover some small distance and keep on breathing, my frog kick does the job. I've had to work at it. Half the trick is to not think of yourself as a sinker. Take in air and let it out, make your way; roll over in the water and rest on your back a moment when you absolutely must. It works in lakes and even, on a calm day, the ocean; it's got me through a job or two; and parenthood so far; also Christmas dinner for a crowd, any number of exams, dozens of fraught conversations.

5. Riding in trucks with girls

Booze was not in play. Darkness, a wind-gust full against the high-riding chassis of a half-ton truck, a come-hither slither of gravel at the shoulder of the road. So much depends on where you sit. Seatbelts, well, we never used them. Everyone knew that in the event of an accident you didn't want to be trapped inside. You wanted to be thrown free. It was my turn to sit by the passenger door. Debra sat between Maddy, who was driving, and me.

Debra: her wispy blond hair; her bitten-back fingernails; her green eyes, small in her face, and pretty; her rare brand of honesty about herself and what she saw around her. Debra, two months short of graduation. She was thrown through the windshield.

Some time after the crash I woke inside the truck, alone. It was parked on its roof. I moved my foot and the brittle plastic shield of the interior light crunched under my running shoe. A muscle-clutch along my back as I crawled through the broken window and up the ditch.

"Debra?!"

"Maddy?!"

Sitting in the fringe of long grass at the edge of the road, I raised an arm to an approaching car. It wasn't my feeble movement but rather the lights of the overturned truck shining askew into the night that alerted the folks who eventually pulled over—the dutiful man who helped me into his car and drove me to the hospital; the kind man who found Maddy and walked her up to a different car; and the man who stayed at the scene, because the dead must not be abandoned. Though we do—once those first raw wrestles with grief and guilt have exhausted us, as memory attenuates, as years pass, we abandon our dead. We leave them behind at any rate, making visits that grow less and less frequent to a forlorn, shallow hollow shaped by the loss of loss. It's a fact that is as howlingly sad as it is necessary; it's how life goes on.

Years onward, these events no longer feel as if they're mine: they belong to Younger Me, an ordinary girl in unexceptional situations. I remember that girl, the town she came from, and the times. I remember she wondered why she was she and not someone else; she wondered what it was like for those others, inside those other bodies, inside those other houses in the town. It's a place I don't go back to, other than in mind. That young girl hands these events up into the present, each one freeze-dried and tightly packaged, oddly unrelated to Me of Now. I take one, slit the covering, peel back the plastic, and before I can feel it with my bare hand, the shape of the thing has changed. The shape, the colour, the temperature, the substance. I look through the drift of steam and dust and wonder at the complicated fortune that's turned Younger Me into Me of Now, with everything so damn lovely and my chair so comfortable and my death either years in the future or just around the corner.

I've done a thorough search of mind and body, and if there's a place inside me, either physical or mental, that retains a remnant of belief that my life was truly at risk in any of these episodes, I can't find it. It's all become abstract, and here's the paradox: on some abstracted theatre stage outside myself I see how any one of these occasions could have been the end of me.

Everyone has such a list, short or long, quiet or dramatic, but what do we the living get from casting back to times we might have died? So much—*so* much—seems random. Once in a while, for an hour or a day I might be mindful that I've had some second chances—second, third, fourth—but it's hard to know what to make of that any more than I know what to make of waking into the world in the first place. Urgency, for me, comes more from other directions than from the notion that, up to now, I've made it through intact. If ever there's urgency in my present life, it comes from love or deadlines; it comes from someone else's need; or from some visceral, often selfish, in-the-moment impulse; or from working not to fail at what's before me; or from nearly falling off a ledge right now, today.

6. At the movies

My memory of the episode begins with the barrel of a .22 coming down the stairs. We were sitting—Younger Me and my friends Judy and Anna, who were sisters—on the couch in Judy and Anna's home, watching the afternoon movie as we did so many Saturdays. That TV was where we went to find a world beyond our own. The parents weren't in the house that day, they were at work, cleaning bunkhouses over by the railway station. From where we sat we three had a view through the living room doorway to the hallway and the lower portion of the staircase and the rifle coming down. The boy who carried the .22 was Judy and Anna's older brother Frank. First we saw his lower legs as he descended, sock feet and jeans; then the rifle barrel; then his naked torso.

That view of the staircase is where this memory begins, but there must have been a lead-up for which I've lost the details. He must have come in earlier from the party that began the night before and carried on well into the day. Maybe his return was uneventful. Maybe he stumbled in soused and sleepy and climbed the stairs, and we heard his door close and his bed creak. He wasn't what you'd call a drunk, but once in a while the guys would party all night without their girls and write the next day off. Boys were boys, and so they should be.

"He's got the .22!" Judy shouted, and we leapt from the couch and scrambled through the dining room and the kitchen and the back porch and out the door. I have it in mind like a still photograph, the image before we leapt: the jeans, the dark barrel, the bare forearms, soft-haired.

We dashed for the alley, where we huddled behind a shed. We heard a shot inside the house. Another. Four shots in all, if I recall correctly, and chances are I don't. Then, a long silence. I don't remember if we talked or cried or simply shook. The silence stretched. Had he managed to do the worst? How, in fact, *would* a person do the worst with a long gun? There are ways, but surely he wasn't sober enough to execute them.

Moments went by. Judy said, "I'm going in."

"Don't, you can't," said Anna, but we hadn't the wherewithal to stop her. We waited, Anna and I. Did we breathe? Did we hold our breath? No shots. Still no shots. And then a sob and the slap-shut of the screen door. I was too frightened to peer around the corner of the shed. Anna, brave Anna, stuck her neck out. "Oh, God!" she said, and then I looked too, past her shoulder: Judy, running, face all tears and snot, hair flying out on either side like tatty wings.

She reached us and we stood there sobbing. We didn't hug each other for comfort; hugging wasn't something girls would do, in that place and time. We were three separate souls a-tremble. I'd been dating the boy with the .22 for almost a year—dating him for reasons I can no longer imagine, nor even for the reason you might expect, because the single lesson my mother delivered in sex education was to say, *If you get pregnant you'll never get out of here.* And that was one effective lesson.

Judy wiped a hand across her nose. "He shot the damn TV!"

What did that mean? That he'd shot the TV, and then he'd shot himself?

"Why would he shoot the damn TV?" Judy said. She slumped

over herself, sobbing, and it penetrated that he was still alive in there. Him and his rifle. Her tears were equal parts relief and anger. A television wasn't easily replaced; you didn't just go out and get another, ba-da-bing-bang. How dare he put us through all this and waste the TV into the bargain?

Even after the shooting stopped, Frank was out of it for hours. He lay on his back on the dining room floor and pushed with his heels until his head jammed against the baseboard. He moaned and muttered and made no sense. He was something other than ordinary soused, or so we certainly thought.

Frank was out of school by then, working in radiator repair, but his sisters and I still rode an overcapacity yellow bus to high school in a larger town. We were ridiculous, said the others on the bus, what with our theory that some ne'er-do-well at the all-night party had dropped a drug into Frank's booze. We couldn't even say what sort of drug it might have been. To and from school we listened as a self-appointed poet laureate of the yellow bus performed a piece of doggerel. To give credit where credit is due, I will mention his facility with meter and his talent for internal rhyme: *James was there with his long hair / and just for a kick he drugged that hick.*

The young poet was bound to make rhymes of our lives, of course he was. This was the best material ever to tumble across his path. And here I am as well, raking through that afternoon all these years on. We're human beings and we do this; we pause and turn and rake through life. And the writing down, writing through, writing over—the record I make of life and acts and accidents in a time and place—I'm not sure what I hope to harmonize. I do love human beings, and I wish the best for Younger Me and the people who surround her, the poet of the yellow bus included.

"Why would he shoot the damn TV?" Judy's question in the alley.

"Because it moved," said Anna. "Because the picture was moving.

178

If we'd stayed in there, *we* would have been the things that moved."
But we didn't stay. Judy shouted, "He's got the .22!" and snapped us
out of our consternation, and we bolted to a safer place.

It didn't happen immediately, but it wasn't long after the
incident with the .22 that I let that boyfriend go. Decades later I
can write this down and end by saying, Life goes on. In lives five
hundred miles apart and different in five hundred ways, life goes
on for Frank and for me. He's still doing the same old shit—that's
how he put it several years ago when he phoned, surreal on a sunny
morning and I took the receiver from my husband, the soil of a
newly turned flower garden under my nails. Still fixing rads, Frank
said, and happy enough about that. He's a good man, I expect.
Anna died of cancer years ago. Judy, last I heard, still lived in the
town where we grew up. She married; she raised a loving family in
the house with the bullets buried in the lath-and-plaster walls. The
girl who was brave enough to go back in.

Paging Kafka's Elegist
Elana Wolff

I FIRST MET Kafka's elegist in the pages of Kafka's diary: the entry for March 25, 1915. He was not an elegist then. He appeared, compressed to initials, as "L. the western Jew who assimilated to the Hasidim"—a branch of Jewish Orthodoxy that holds mysticism and simple piety as fundamental to the faith. In the same entry, a few lines forward, he appeared again—as "G. in a caftan"; that is, G. in the long cloak of Hasidic garb. In Kafka's entry for March 25th he is both L. and G. —L. for Langer and G. for Georg. His full name, reflecting a complexity of identity, was Georg (Jiří) Mordechai (Dov) Langer: Georg, German for George; Jiří, the same in Czech; Mordechai, his Hebrew name; Dov, his second Hebrew name; and Langer—the family name. He used all five, depending on context.

Georg Mordechai Langer (1894-1943) is not a household name and I would not have known it, if not for Franz Kafka (1883-1924). I was drawn to Kafka's fraught world as a teen; first I read *The Metamorphosis*, then *The Trial*, both of which link to the year Kafka and Langer met and became friends. 1915 was the year *The Metamorphosis* was published. It was also the year *The Trial* was abandoned, unfinished—only to be released posthumously at the initiative of Kafka's and Langer's mutual friend, Max Brod (1884-

1968). But this was not known to me then. I read Kafka uninitiated, on my own—without background information or guidance of a teacher, mentor, syllabus, or classroom. Somehow I was brought to Kafka, and became wrapped in his wry, maddening, precise yet parabolic world. His fictions were irresistible. They've proven to be inexhaustible also. One returns to Kafka, and reads him through the works of others. Kafka has not only suffused literature and art of the last century, he became a byword for the time.

A hundred years ago, when Kafka and Langer met, Kafka was not yet KAFKA. He was not yet thirty-three. His publication credits were few, his writing known only to a small group of discerning readers. But "there was no need of his works," wrote Max Brod in his 1937 *Franz Kafka: A Biography*, "the man produced his own effect, simply by virtue of his personality, his occasional remarks and his conversation. Despite all the shyness of his behavior, he was always recognized by men of worth as someone out of the ordinary"—though his day-résumé outlines a man typical of his station and time. He achieved his law degree at Prague's Charles University and was employed for most of his working life as an insurance adjuster at the semi-governmental Worker's Accident Insurance Institute in Prague's Old Town—near the Square where he was born, raised, schooled, and where his parents owned and ran a successful fancy goods store.

The literary fruit of Kafka's short life—lived for the most part within a taut two-mile radius— rankled me. I couldn't love it and couldn't give it up. I've dwelled in many places, let go of many books, but I still have the $5.95, 1976 Schocken paperback edition of *Kafka, The Complete Stories*—now held together with elastic bands—that I took on my first trip to Israel and read and reread during my year there. Kafka—who never wrote the word Jew in any of his fiction— became part of my Jewish awakening. I felt the Jewishness in his catholic writing before I knew the fullness of it.

In 2010 I chose Kafka as my subject for a final presentation-assignment in a biography course I was taking; he was a natural choice. Throughout fall and winter and into spring 2011, I pored over his oeuvre anew—the stories, the novels. Also the notebooks, diaries, letters, critical literature and biographies—in search of threads and motifs in his lifeline, their metamorphoses through cycles and crises, and a picture of how his life intentions were or were not met.

A key theme of Kafka's biography is the centrality of friendship to his literary development and posthumous fame and acclaim. Particularly the uncommon friendship of Max Brod. The two came from the same assimilated German-Jewish, middle-class Prague background and met at the Charles University—both aspiring writers, both studying law. They connected quickly over love of argument and literature. Early in their friendship Brod introduced Kafka to others who would also have an impact on the author, including his muse and two-time fiancée Felice Bauer (1887-1960), whom he never married, and first publisher Kurt Wolff (1887-1963); later, Georg Mordechai Langer.

Brod encouraged and promoted Kafka throughout his lifetime and as his literary executor famously saved his friend's unpublished work from incineration, disavowing Kafka's will that everything be burned unread. Instead, Brod negotiated and prepared for publication Kafka's three unfinished novels—*The Trial* in 1925, *The Castle* in 1926, and *Amerika* in 1927. He secured his friend's manuscripts and advocated on behalf of his literary legacy. He edited and arranged publication of much of his private writing as well—the diaries, the massive body of correspondence; also stories, sketches, and reflections. No doubt, without the intercession of Max Brod, Kafka would not be known as he is today.

Brod was Georg Mordechai Langer's literary executor too. Max Brod had a life and post-death impact on both of his Prague friends. "Georg Langer," named as such, is threaded into a half-page of Brod's biography of Kafka: "I used to spend a lot of time, together with my cabalistic friend Georg Langer, at the house of a miracle-working rabbi, a refugee from Galicia who lived in dark, unfriendly, crowded rooms in the Prague suburb Žižkov. Unusual circumstances of life had brought me near to a kind of religious fanaticism…It is worthy of note that Franz, whom I took with me to a 'Third Meal' at the close of the Sabbath…remained, I must admit, very cool. He was undoubtedly moved by the age-old sounds of an ancient folk life, but…Franz had his own personal mysticism, he couldn't take over from others a ready-made ritual." This passage, likely drawn from Brod's own diary, parallels Kafka's diary entry recording the same Sabbath visit. Brod might have said more about Langer, more about Franz and Langer… more about the three-way friendship. He had what to say. But his slant on his Kafka's legacy was so specific, his focus on his best friend so close, that anything outside the aura of that aperture was minimized. Not without reason, Brod's biography of Kafka has been faulted for crossing into hagiography.

Franz himself saw his own character as deeply, probably irredeemably flawed. He sought perfection in writing, but was harassed by lifelong hypochondria and intermittent self-loathing. It's generally thought that he suffered from clinical depression. Writing was a necessity, essential to his sense of being. And while providing a measure of pleasure, release, and consolation, his work also records the struggle out of which it emerged. In this respect, he and Georg Langer were not unalike.

I did not include Langer in my June, 2011 presentation of Kafka. The information I had was sketchy. But a short entry in *A Franz Kafka Encyclopedia* claiming that Langer's "importance in Kafka's life was largely overlooked" continued to intrigue me. As did the reference in the *Encyclopedia* (and elsewhere) to an elegy for Kafka, written by Langer in Hebrew and published in a small collection at the Prague Jewish printing works in1929. I was eager to find the book, which proved not to be easy, and to know more about the Kafka-Langer connection.

My quest began with a more thorough reading of Kafka's *Diaries* and *Letters*. There are five references to Langer in the *Diaries*—four in 1915, one in 1920. The 1915 entries all cover Jewish topics: Langer the Hasid; the Sabbath visit with Langer and Max to the home of the Žižkov Rabbi; excerpts of Langer's Hasidic stories. A one-line entry on October 1920 records a visit to Kafka at his parents' home—"first Langer, then Max." Kafka had been diagnosed with tuberculosis in August 1917 and by 1920 his health was in decline.

There are also five references to Langer in Kafka's *Letters*— two from Marienbad in July 1916. Kafka spent ten days at the Bohemian resort with his then-fiancée Felice Bauer and Langer happened to be there at the same time, with the entourage of the ailing Rabbi of Belz. The two friends met up for long evening walks (somewhat surprising, seeing that Kafka was holidaying with his fiancée). A long letter to Max details the walks and time spent with Langer; a shorter letter to another mutual friend, Felix Weltsch (1884-1964), also comments on the walks. Langer appears next in a postcard sent to Max in November 1917 from Zürau in the Czech countryside. Kafka was then taking his first leave of absence from work after the TB diagnosis and was resting in the care of his youngest sister Ottla on their brother-in-law's farm. The note addresses the possibility of Franz securing work for Langer in the Kafka family business; nothing came of it. In spring of 1920 Kafka was taking a rest-cure in Meran in the South Tyrol. In a reply to Felix Weltsch, Kafka writes of a "childish" "giddy" "gladness" that he is "shamelessly given to" with respect to something Langer had conveyed about Kafka to Weltsch. Whatever it was, is not spelled out. And the last mention of Langer appears in a letter to Max Brod, written from a sanatorium in the Tatra Mountains of Slovakia in December1920. The reference is to Langer's having formed a *Mizrachi* group in Prague, indicating by this time his commitment to religious Zionism.

The ten references to Langer in Kafka's *Diaries* and *Letters* point to an ongoing connection over a span of years; they do not seem to indicate a particularly intimate bond—at least not from Kafka's perspective. The one mention that stands out for ambiguousness of tone is the message to Langer sent through Weltsch in spring of 1920. The "childish" "giddy" "gladness" juxtaposed to "shamelessness" is curiously coy; it's hard to know what to make of it.

From Kafka's writing alone one would not know that Langer was also a writer. In fact, Langer began publishing articles in Czech and German in1919, published his first poems in Hebrew in 1923, and that same year, the year before Kafka's death—published with Diederichs of Münich—a psychoanalytic study titled *Die Erotik der Kabbala* (*The Eroticism of Kabbala*). He became a prolific author. In addition to small books, essays and articles on a variety of subjects, in 1937 he published with Elk of Prague, *Devět bran* (*Nine Gates*)—a collection of Hasidic tales of wonder-working rabbis, the likes of which Kafka had heard from Langer and recounted in his diary in 1915. In July 2011 I located *Nine Gates*—first published in English translation in 1961 by James Clark of London—at the York University Library in Toronto, and read it with great interest. The stories not only provide a fascinating window into a devout Eastern European Jewish world, now vanished. The Foreword to the collection, titled "My Brother Jiří," writtten by Langer's older brother František Langer (1888-1965) for the English edition, contains the most extensive biography available on Langer. Though, like Max Brod's biography of Kafka, František's Foreword (as would become clear), carries an audible slant.

Jiří (Georg Mordechai) was born in the Prague suburb of Královské Vinohrady, the youngest of three sons. The Langers, like the Kafkas and Brods, were westernized, middle-class Jews. Langer senior was a shopkeeper, a practical man, minimally observant. (Langer's mother, "poor thing" František writes, "was deaf.") "Father," as he is referred to, favoured Czech over German (the dominant language of Prague Jewry), belonged to the patriotic Sokol sport movement, and unlike Kafka's and Brod's fathers, sent his sons to Czech schools. František, the eldest, followed the trajectory of his father's assimilation, becoming a chief physician in the Czech army during World War One, and later an acclaimed Czech-nationalist playwright. Josef, the middle brother, joined the family business. Jiří, described as a lonely boy who was reading Czech mystical poetry by age fifteen, became "infected" with enthusiasm for mysticism by way of his friend Alfred Fuchs. The two learned Hebrew and read Jewish literature together. Fuchs converted to Catholicism and the friendship broke off. Jiří immersed himself in the study of Torah, Talmud, and Hebrew (for which he had a gift), quit school, and at the age of nineteen in 1913 set out for Belz, Eastern Galicia, and the Hasidic court of Rabbi Yissachar Dov Rokeach (1851-1926).

Apart from a few breaks, Langer lived five years in the Hasidic world and became thoroughly versed in its ways and faith. Kafka and Langer met in early 1915 when Langer was back in Prague. He'd been drafted into the Austrian army, then discharged for refusing to obey orders that contravened his religious observance. Kafka and Brod were both exempted from military duty—Brod for medical reasons and Kafka on grounds that he was indispensable to the Worker's Accident Insurance Institute. The Langer family, by František's account, were deeply distressed by Jiří's Hasidic conversion and "exhibitionism" upon his first return from Belz. František likens the Langer family situation to that of the Samsa family in Kafka's *The Metamorphosis*. In both cases—the real and the fictional—the cozy family nest is upended by a 'monstrosity.' The Samsas ultimately dispose of their son and brother, once he's fully dehumanized and deceased. At least, says František, the Langers were "practical," and sought the help of a sensitive local rabbi to persuade Jiří to modify his ways. František writes that he himself never met Franz Kafka, but that his brother and Kafka became friends during the War: "Kafka evidently found in Jiří a *kindred spirit* (my emphasis) and the two used to go for walks together in Prague."

So what was the kindredness? What did Kafka find in Jiří; Jiří in Kafka? No doubt part of the attraction was mutual interest in an authentic non-Western Jewish experience. Both were contemptuous of the "insufficient scrap" of Judaism, as Kafka put it, practiced by Western Jewry. Langer found authenticity in Galicia, within the strictures of the Yiddish-speaking Hasidic court. Kafka found his version of Jewish authenticity in Prague, by way of a Yiddish theatre troupe from Galicia. The *Diaries* include some thirty entries on the troupe that performed in Prague from 1911 to 1913—descriptions of the actors, synopses of the plays, critiques of the performances. Kafka saw in the passion of the actors and their naturalistic plays a living, breathing Judaism, and he connected with it. Aspects of the mystical, the folkloric, and the parabolic were common to both men's quests from the pre-war period forward, though Kafka remained cool to Jewish religious study until his last years. Both were also interested in Yiddish and Langer became fluent early in his stay at Belz. Langer, gifted at languages, knew Hebrew prior to the War; Kafka did not. It's quite possible that Langer's knowledge and great love of the old-new tongue sparked in Kafka the will to learn Hebrew as well.

Langer left the Belz community for good at the war's end and went to Vienna to study at the Hebrew Pedagogic Academy. When he returned to Prague, he supported himself by teaching Hebrew and Jewish studies and working in clerical capacity for Zionist organizations. To the relief of František and the family, he'd given up his Hasidic garb and assumed a more "normal attitude," but he remained religious and to their new chagrin had taken up study of Freud and his disciples and had begun to use psychoanalytic methods in analyzing sources of Jewish ritual, mysticism, and the religious idea. (This interest resulted in the publication of *Die Erotik der Kabbala* in 1923.)

As for Kafka, he surreptitiously took up Hebrew study during the war. It came as a revelation to Max that by December 1917, Kafka had worked his way through forty-five lessons of the formidable textbook of the time, *Hebrew Grammar and Reader for Schools and Self-Instruction*, by Moses Rath. In a rare instance of censure, Brod writes of his friend, "So he was trying me out when he asked me some time ago, with every appearance of innocence, how do you count in Hebrew. This making a big secret of everything. There is something very great about it, but also something evil." Kafka was evidently serious about his Hebrew study and in spring 1918 asked Langer to give him private lessons. A note in Max Brod's collection of Kafka's *Letters to Friends, Family and Editors* records that in fall of 1921 Brod and Kafka took Hebrew lessons from Langer together as well. The revival of Hebrew as a living language was one of the important steps towards creating a Jewish State, and as such, fundamentally tied to Zionism. Did Kafka's diligence in learning Hebrew mean that he, like Brod and Langer, became a Zionist? Like so many questions about Kafka, this is hard to answer unequivocally.

František closes his Foreword to *Nine Gates* by relating how he escaped Prague in1939, first to France then to England, where he settled. Josef chose suicide over the prospect of imposed death. (Like Kafka's parents, though not his sisters, František's parents died before the war.) In 1939 Jiří escaped Prague for Palestine along the Danube-to-Istanbul route. (Max Brod also escaped Prague for Palestine—on the last train before the borders were closed—carrying Kafka's manuscripts in his suitcase.) Jiří contracted nephritis during the tortuous passage; it became chronic and led to his premature death in Tel Aviv in 1943. During these last years, living in the Land, he was frequently too ill to work. He received a small grant for refugees and some assistance from František—"once difficulties from the war had been overcome." He turned to translating his Hasidic tales into Hebrew and resumed writing Hebrew poetry. Max Brod and Jiří were friends to the end. František relates that as his brother lay dying, Max brought him the proof-sheets of his second book of poems—"written in Palestine." Brod also arranged Langer's funeral, attended to his literary estate, and helped oversee the posthumous publication of his second small collection, titled *Me'at Tsori* (*A Little Balsam*).

I was unable to locate Langer's poetry in Toronto or online. In August 2011 my husband David and I were in Israel. I hoped to find a copy of Langer's first book of poetry—cited by František as *Piyyutim ve-Shirei Yedidut* (*Poems and Songs of Friendship*)—in one of the used- or rare-book stores, and came up empty-handed. We did find the title in the National Library system—at the Givat Ram campus of The Hebrew University in Jerusalem—but the book was in storage and we were told it would take several days to locate, if it could be located at all. The day before our departure, we received email notification that the book had been retrieved and was on hold at the Judaica Reading Room.

I did not know that the physicality of a book could make me so emotional. Standing under the high light of the dry and quiet room, I held the little original in my hands like a first-time mother; touched the simple cardboard cover. The author's name, printed in thin Hebrew letters above the title—*Piyyutim ve-Shirei Yedidot*—different, I noticed, by one letter, from what František had written in his Foreword to *Nine Gates*. The contents under the cover—sixteen poems listed in triangular configuration. The place of publication—Prague. Year—1929, in Hebrew letters, not numerals. Publisher—Dr. Josef Fläsch. I was holding one of a small edition that Langer had surely brought with him on his long escape from Prague in 1939 and bequeathed to the library in 1943. A great wave welled up inside me. There was not a single due-date stamped on the sign-out slip pasted to the right-hand side of the next page. I turned each page carefully and stopped when I came to the twelfth poem, "On the Death of the Poet—after Franz Kafka," the name printed plainly under the title. It was the elegy. I had found what I'd come for and knew in the moment that I would read these pieces deeply, and together with David, translate them faithfully.

David was a hesitant partner in the search, until then. Once we found the book and started to read the pieces, he too was pulled in. The poems that opened out to us were the work of an expert Hebraist; poems richly informed by Biblical and Kabbalistic sources. Liturgical in style and craft, modern in theme and prospect. It soon became clear that these were intensely personal poems— of passion, agitation, longing, spiritual reaching, loneliness, and unreciprocated homo-romantic love; written male to male.

Franz Kafka is the only person named in the collection, which does not mean that Kafka is the subject of all the poems. But it seemed to us that he was implicit in more than one—based on descriptions, allusions, and juxtaposition. The elegy itself is an expression of exalted and impassioned love beyond death, as exemplified in the lines: "The water-fire-air, the animate-plant-inanimate / join with me together, who were estranged from me till now; with every expression of kindness they lend me a hand, caressing me genteelly and behold you are among them!...Place between my breasts the weight of your shadowed soul / and the dream of your bones, lay down on my pillow's softness." And following the elegy is the poem "Alone," in which "I did not press you to my breast, / my arms did not envelop you, / and that my heart was all aflame / I did not tell you / with my mouth, I could not. / And now you are gone, / and nothing is left / but the remembering / and regret..." "Like the Dying Inside" speaks of "tremours of a secret love / you dare not / love / to the end." And "The Strength in Splendour" announces "my belovèd"..."his comely face"...the "pearls shower from his mouth," then "grief: a tear...and trembling..." There was no way of knowing who Langer had addressed in more than one of his love poems, and whether Franz Kafka was the one great love among others, but it seemed possible.

What was certain: Georg Mordechai Langer's disclosure of his deepest leanings through his poetry was a daring act of self-expression. Given that he was religious, too, he would have been living with immense inner pressure—that of making meaning of his sexual identity in light of his commitment to Judaism, which proscribes same-sex relations. If the repeat expression of unfulfilled love in his poems is an indication, however, Langer did not act on his desires. The poems were a channel for his feelings of both ecstasy and rejection; a release, a replacement, and a consolation. In one of his most unshielded pieces he writes: "Only my poetry is an escape, my lamentation, my refuge."

Once our translation was underway, I began to see František's Foreword with different eyes. The family "horror"-narrative over Jiří's religious "ostentation" and the disparagement of his "innocent" yet "blasphemous" psychoanalytic writing, could have been František's masking of a deeper, more shameful family secret. Anyone who was close to Langer and anyone who read his poetry would have known his truth.

In the fall of 2011 I pitched the idea of a bilingual edition of Langer's collection to my publisher. The editor-in-chief, a Kafka enthusiast, was intrigued by the idea of having the first translation of an elegy to Kafka on the press. So much has been published on Kafka, yet somehow the elegy had remained obscured. It was like a piece from the ethers, and the back story added appeal. But a bilingual Hebrew/English work had never been done by the press, and there would be challenges. Then came the synchronous stroke: the submission by an American author of a new translation of two late story collections by Kafka, *A Country Doctor* (1919) and *A Hunger Artist* (1924). Langer and Kafka arrived at the press together. As it turned out, the two books were released under one cover in 2014, in an inventive flipside format. Given the Kafka-Langer link, the two-in-one solution was brilliant. But I'm getting ahead of myself.

During the course of reading, researching, drafting, discussing, writing and rewriting our translations, David and I (I felt) were coming into a new closeness. We'd never done this kind of work together and it brought out qualities in our individualities that had not met in the open. One day David set his pen on the kitchen table—beside the papers, notebooks, Hebrew texts, dictionaries, and tea cups—and said he felt we were doing the work of *ilui neshama*—elevation of the soul. By translating the poems of Mordechai Langer we were giving them new breath, we were demonstrating a continuing impact of Langer's life and deeds in the world, we were elevating his soul, together. I had not heard David speak this way before, and could only listen.

We'd been living with the intimacy of Langer's poems for a year and a half when we next returned to Israel. We made a point of fitting into our schedule a visit to Langer's grave at the Nachalat Yitzchak Cemetery on the outskirts of Tel Aviv. Founded in 1932, the cemetery contains more than 30,000 graves, including mass graves for unidentified soldiers, graves of children, graves of cultural and political figures, graves of Rebbes of Hasidic dynasties, memorials to communities lost in the Holocaust, and re-interred ashes. We had no idea where to find Langer in this dense and sprawling resting place. We entered the low white office building inside the main gate to ask for assistance. It was a bright, clear, chilly day at the end of February 2013.

The custodian, a pale man with a large black yarmulka, reddish beard, and long curly side-locks, could have fit František's description of Jiří himself when he first returned from Belz. The man was amiable, eager to help. We spoke in Hebrew. We told him we were looking for the grave of Georg Mordechai Langer. He tapped the name into his computer and came up with the information: Area 41: Row 24: Number 21. "Where are you from?" he asked us. "Canada," we told him. "You must have come for the *yahrzeit*," he said. (*Yahrzeit* is the Yiddish word for the anniversary of a person's death.) "It was just his *yahrzeit*, are you family?" he asked. "No, we're not family. We didn't realize it was his *yahrzeit*. We were here and we wanted to visit his grave," we told him. "I'll take you there," he said, "You won't easily find it on your own." He led us along the narrow lanes, the tightly crowded tracts. When we arrived, we were silent in seeing the simple inscription: *Ha-Meshorer* (The Poet) Mordechai Langer and below his name the date of his death. There were three stones on the grave. People had visited and placed them there—as is the way when visiting a Jewish grave. "You're not family?" he asked again quizzically. "No," said David, "we're admirers." (The word sounded odd.) "He was a poet, a friend of Franz Kafka," David continued. "You know, Kafka..." "No," said the man, "never heard of him." The three of us stood there. Then he asked us if we would like him to recite a psalm. We could have done this ourselves but since he asked, we said yes. He recited Psalm 130. We listened. Afterwards, he returned us to the cemetery entrance. We thanked him, tipped him for his service, and left. We hardly knew what to say to one another. We'd been so nonplused by the experience, we'd forgotten to place stones on the grave to mark our visit.

David had the painstaking work of resetting the Hebrew poems—with their complex medieval-style vowel notations. We wanted the originals to correspond line-by-line, too, with the translations, on facing pages. This required a combined effort of precision, as did composing the notes on the individual pieces. I wrote the Introduction, including the back story to the project, and a Note on the Translation process. Nothing was quick. And we were grappling with puzzles, hunches, and corrections along the way.

The matter of the title was resistant. František cited *Piyyutim ve-Shirei Yedidut* in his Foreword, which translates as *Poems and Songs of Friendship*. I'd seen this rendering in a few other references to the collection as well. But as soon as I set eyes on the original book, I noticed that the last word of the title was actually *Yedidot*, not *Yedidut*. At first I didn't attribute to this much significance. In Hebrew, this is only a difference of one small vowel-dot, and the more common word is *yedidut*—meaning "friendship." However, the less common word—*yedidot*, together with *shirei*—meaning "songs"—translates as "love songs." The term *shirei yedidot* appears in the liturgical song, *Shir Ha-Kavod*—"Song of Glory," attributed to Rabbi Judah the Hasid (1150-1217). Langer was a supreme Hebraist and he knew his liturgy. He had surely chosen his source and worded his title carefully to say what he intended. For months, David and I proceeded under the working title *Poems and Songs of Friendship*. But the more we lived with Langer's language and sources and the content of his poems, the more we understood that he really had not written poems of friendship—a non-romantic, mutual relationship. He had written poems of romantic desire, longing, dejection, and loneliness: unrequited love songs.

I closed my Note on Translation with a gloss on our decision to title our English translation *Poems and Songs of Love*. But another point in František's Foreword continued to needle me. František wrote that as Jiří lay dying, Max Brod brought him the proof-sheets of the book containing the Hebrew poems he'd written in Palestine: *Me'at Tsori* (*A Little Balsam*), published posthumously in Tel Aviv in 1943. František relates that Jiří writes fondly of Prague and the Old-New Synagogue in these poems, and with "rapturous adoration" about the "beauty of the Palestinian countryside," but "not a great deal about people." It struck me that František should have this much to say about the content of Jiří's second collection when he'd said next to nothing about the first, which was in fact a great deal about people.

Initially, I'd been drawn to the first collection only—because of the elegy for Kafka. But entering into Langer's life as we had, through translating his poems, altered things—even something between ourselves. And I knew we would be remiss if we didn't seek and read the second collection. I had questions too. I was interested to see if, in addition to paeans to the Land and reminiscences on Prague, there were new romantic poems among the few "about people" that František alluded to. More so, I was curious to see if any of the pieces from the first collection had been reprinted in the second. František made no mention of this, but I had a hunch that Langer might have decided to bring his dearest pieces forward, to be part of his last legacy in a book published in the Land of his dreams.

Our materials were to be submitted by the end of February, 2014—to allow enough preparation time for a fall release of the book. The poems were ready. The Introduction, the notes on the poems, and the Note on Translation were also written. But I was living with puzzles and hunches when David and I visited Israel in January 2014, a month before our work was due. This time I was hoping to find an original copy of Langer's second book, at the historic Beit Ariela Library in Tel Aviv. We were thrilled to hear from the Israel Collection librarian that *Me'at Tsori* (*A Little Balsam*) was in the stacks and available to us to peruse as non-members. But what we found was not a copy of Langer's little original. Rather, a 286-page volume of Mordechai (Dov) Langer's *Collected Writings in Hebrew*—a 1984 edition compiled by Israeli poet/academic Miriam Dror, including a biographical preface by Professor Dov Sadan (1902-1989), photos, letters, Hasidic tales, Langer's two collections of poems, prose pieces, and Dror's MA thesis on Langer's poetry.

There was so much to surprise and delight—most exciting of all a short prose piece by Langer titled "Something about Kafka" (*"Mashehu al-Kafka"*), originally published in the Tel Aviv journal *Hegeh* (*Voice*) in February 1941 at the request of then-editor, Dov Sadan. Nowhere in anything I'd read on Kafka or Langer had I seen reference to this astonishing piece in Hebrew. We read it word for word on the spot and I knew that a translation had to be included in our book.

"Something about Kafka" establishes a deeper, closer Kafka-Langer tie than is portrayed in other published sources. It confirms that the two spent quotidian time together "for a full medley of years"—walking, talking, learning, riding the city rails together and speaking in Hebrew. "Unlike the other Prague Zionists," Langer writes, Kafka "spoke a fluent Hebrew"; they spoke Hebrew to one another, and Kafka took "heartfelt pride" in his knowledge of the language. "Though Kafka maintained he was not a Zionist," says Langer, "he deeply envied those who fulfilled the great principle of

Zionism, bodily; that is, the principle of immigrating to the Land of Israel." Langer also confirms what I could not know from what is available in Kafka's *Diaries*, *Letters* and other sources, but could only infer from circumstance and context; namely, that Kafka *did* know Langer wrote poetry, and in fact read and understood what it said. Langer refers to the publication of his first poems that appeared in the Warsaw literary journal *Kolot* (*Voices*) in 1923: "Kafka said to me that they resemble, a little, Chinese poetry. So I went and purchased for myself a collection of Chinese poetry in French translation…and from then on this delightful book never left my table." This reference affirmed my hunch that there was indeed a Kafka-connection to Langer's poem "On the Poems of Li-Tai-Pei," which appears immediately before the elegy in *Poems and Songs of Love*. Langer was evidently inspired, by Kafka's indication, to write the "Chinese poem" and he placed it next to the elegy because of the connection. I'd also been struck by the inverse symmetry of the two poems. In both pieces Langer waxes exultant and woeful to evoke union and disunion. In the 'Chinese poem' he opens with exultation—"a heavenly voice from the depths," the "intoxicating scents of summer"—and closes on a note of sadness, thwarted in understanding and "bitter as the world and everything in it." In the elegy he begins with "the bond is at an end, / "a bond made of waves of the sea of the world." There is "wailing and ululation," due to the "turn" (Kafka's decease), but true union does not end with the disunion of death; for Langer, incorporeal Kafka remains present in the very elements. If there is to be "jubilant" joining of "free men," however, it will be "in the bosom of the universe. / On the fount from which together life and death as brothers spring." Not in this life, not in these bodies.

In tone, content, and allusion, "Something about Kafka" affirms Langer's awe of Kafka. Kafka is the "great and wondrous personality" in whose "shadow" he, Langer, "dwelled." Langer does not paint the relationship as equal, in the way of regular friendship. His declaration: "Hardly a day goes by that I do not call up his memory before me" indicates a deeper-than-friend intensity. And while his memories of Kafka may be reliable, Langer maintains restraint. Not everything he remembers will he reveal. He acknowledges Kafka's secrecy, and his will and right to conceal, even in revealing. With Kafka there's paradox. There's nothing specific in "Something about Kafka" to identify Kafka as Langer's great unrequited love. Yet neither is there anything to negate it.

Another of my hunches was validated by the Dror book as well. Langer had indeed included in his second book of poems, *Me'at Tsori* (*A Little Balsam*), pieces from *Poems and Songs of Love* (*Piyyutim ve-Shirei Yedidot*), published fourteen years earlier. And the five poems he chose to reissue in the Land are a significant statement: "On the Poems of Li-Tai-Pei" and "On the Death of the Poet—after Franz Kafka," placed one before the other, as in the first collection. Two of the poems first published in the Warsaw journal *Kolot* in 1923 that Kafka told Langer reminded him of Chinese poetry, both of which expound Langer's sadness in being unfulfilled in his deepest romantic leanings. And the poem, "Like the Dying Inside," set to the Eastern European tune for chanting the biblical Book of *Lamentations*, that ends with "tremours of a secret love / you dare not / love / to the end."

The theme of the secret also comes up in one of the poems "about people" in *Me'at Tsori* (*A Little Balsam*) that František alluded to in his Foreword: true to report, most of the pieces in Langer's second collection are patriotic panegyrics. There are only a few "about people" (which might have been František's mask for homo-romantic poems). One is a short lament from which the title of the collection is drawn, recalling lines written on the margins of a song to a male companion. And the last line of the adjacent poem, titled "Hidat Lila" ("Night Mystery"), contains the line "A secret I will not reveal," which corresponds to what Langer says about Kafka in his prose piece "Something about Kafka," written in the same period as the poem: "He simply did not want to be revealed. He wanted to, but did not want to. He reached out and didn't reach. And he succeeded in both objectives."

Langer, too, lived with duality. He, too, wanted to reveal and be revealed for who he was in his deepest being, and he did this in his poems. But he also concealed. And we found this concealment extended to Miriam Dror's thesis on Langer's work as well. Dror names among Langer's themes: man and his place in the world, the lyrical religious experience, life and death, and, predominantly, loneliness. She holds that Langer's loneliness stemmed from his inability to conform to societal norms, which is reminiscent of František's language. It was striking to us that an academic study should distinguish itself by virtually skirting one of the most essential and certainly most daring aspect of the subject's work. To us this seemed akin to not acknowledging that the emperor has no clothes: the obvious carefully and purposefully undiscussed.

We returned to the Nachalat Yitzchak Cemetery during our January, 2014 visit. This time we knew where to find Langer's resting place. We made our way through the narrow lanes and crowded tracts and stood again before the grave. Again we gazed at the simple inscription: *Ha-Meshorer*—the Poet Mordechai Langer. This is how he wished to be remembered—as a Hebrew poet. He'd written perhaps thousands of pages of prose and criticism and journalism; he'd published fewer than forty poems. Yet these he considered his definitive work—his poems were where his heart lay. Of these pieces, five were dear enough to be chosen twice, and among these, two at least, connected with certainty to Kafka. I looked up from my thoughts, and who should be standing in the row of graves before us but the pale custodian with the large black yarmulka, reddish beard, and long curly side-locks. He looked at us and we looked at him. "It's the Canadians," he announced. "Yes," we said, "you remember us." We were surprised—there are 30,000 graves at Nachalat Yitzchak and the man must see hundreds of people pass through the cemetery each day. What are the chances he'd be standing in the row behind Langer's grave precisely when we arrived. "We brought our prayer book this time," we told him. He nodded, we smiled, he went back to his business. David recited the designated psalms. And this time we placed stones on the grave to mark our visit.

Locating Miriam Dror's *Me'at Tsori* collection of Langer's Hebrew works when we did was crucial. It provided a number of answers, also pages for further investigation. I included an Afterword along with our translation of "Something about Kafka" in the February 2014 submission. So far we haven't made contact with Miriam Dror. This remains something we'd like to do. There's what to discuss. More to be written. And parallel work is ongoing. American LGBT Judaic Studies historian Shaun Jacob Halper has taken up the question of how Langer used sexological and psychological knowledge to articulate a specifically Jewish identity, focusing on the question of why homosexuality became for Langer a modern Jewish question. Nurit Pagi-Lavon, at the University of Haifa, is writing her doctoral dissertation on Max Brod. In 2012, a complicated and protracted legal proceeding ended with the decision of the Tel Aviv District Family Court to transfer the collection of manuscripts written by Franz Kafka and Max Brod from private hands to the Israel National Library in Jerusalem.[1] The trove of handwritten material being inventoried will keep researchers busy for years, and what emerges

---

1 Since the publication of this essay, on August 7, 2016, the Israel Supreme Court rejected an appeal by the heirs of Max Brod to retain the papers.

could shed new light on a number of extraordinary relationships, including the Kafka-Langer.

Our two-in-one flipside book was launched in Toronto in September of 2014. It is now in its second printing. Evidently, there's interest in a new translation of Kafka's late stories, and in a first bilingual translation of Mordechai Langer's love poems; the two together, the story of a quest. There's fascination with relationship—with the threads of the said and the unsaid in it, the written and veiled on the page, the seen and concealed, the revealed and what it conceals. The purposing of concealment and what it keeps.

Author Biographies

CARLEIGH BAKER is a Métis/Icelandic writer. Her work has appeared in *subTerrain*, *PRISM International*, *Joyland*, and *The Journey Prize Anthology*. Her first book, a collection of short stories titled *Bad Endings*, is forthcoming with Anvil Press in spring 2017. She is the current editor of Joyland Vancouver.

GRAEME BAYLISS is a freelance journalist based in Toronto whose writing frequently appears in such publications as *Maisonneuve*, *The Walrus*, *Spacing*, and *Reader's Digest*. He has previously worked as a managing editor of *The Walrus* and an associate editor of *Torontoist*. He mostly enjoys writing about mental health, science, and architecture. He been nominated for a pair of National Magazine Awards.

DESMOND COLE is an award-winning journalist and activist. His work appears in such journals as *The Walrus*, *Toronto Life*, *VICE*, *NOW Magazine*, and *Ethnic Aisle*, and focuses primarily on social justice, equity, immigration, systemic racism, and poverty. Desmond is a columnist for *The Toronto Star* and a radio host on Toronto's Newstalk1010. He is currently writing a book about Black Canada.

KRISTA FOSS' debut novel *Smoke River* (McClelland & Stewart in 2014) was shortlisted for the North American Hammett Prize for literary excellence in crime writing and won the Hamilton Literary Award. Her short fiction has been published in several literary journals and twice been a finalist for The Journey Prize. Her essay writing has been nominated for a National Magazine Award. She lives and writes in Hamilton, Ontario.

DON GILLMOR is the author of three novels, *Kanata, Mount Pleasant*, and *Long Change*. He is also the author of a two-volume history of Canada, *Canada: A People's History*, and three other books of non-fiction as well as nine books for children. His work has appeared in *Rolling Stone, GQ, Walrus, Saturday Night, The Globe and Mail*, and *The Toronto Star*. He lives in Toronto.

WAYNE A. HUNT is Professor of Politics and International Relations at Mount Allison University. He has held visiting academic appointments at the Centre for International Studies at the London School of Economics, at Harvard's Kennedy School and at St. Antony's College, Oxford. He has published in a wide range of areas, including political leadership, grand strategy, communications, and human adaption to technological change.

MICHELLE KAESER is a writer living in Vancouver. Her essays and stories have appeared in publications across the country, including *Maisonneuve, This Magazine, Grain, Prairie Fire, The New Quarterly*, and *The Feathertale Review*, among others. She also writes a blog called "What in the World?!" about interesting facts and stories from around the globe.

RICHARD KELLY KEMICK's poetry and prose have been published in literary magazines and journals across Canada and the United States, most recently in *The Walrus, Maisonneuve*, and *The Fiddlehead*. His debut collection of poetry, *Caribou Run*, was published March 2016 by Goose Lane Editions and selected by CBC as one of the season's Must Read collections.

SUSAN OLDING is the author of *Pathologies: A Life in Essays*, selected by *49th Shelf* and Amazon.ca as one of 100 Canadian books to read in a lifetime. Her writing has won a National Magazine Award and two Edna Awards, among other honours. She lives in Kingston, Ontario, where she is a currently a PhD candidate in the Cultural Studies program at Queen's University.

RICHARD POPLAK is the author of *The Sheikh's Batmobile*; *Ja, No, Man*; *Kenk: A Graphic Portrait*; and *Braking Bad: Chasing Lance Armstrong and the Cancer of Corruption*, an ebook. See more at richardpoplak.com.

MICHAEL ROWE won the 2008 Randy Shilts Nonfiction Prize for his second essay collection, *Other Men's Sons*. He is the author of two novels, *Enter, Night* and *Wild Fell*, which was a finalist for the 2013 Shirley Jackson Award. His essays and journalism have appeared in the *National Post*, *The Globe & Mail*, *SHARP*, *The Advocate*, and the *Huffington Post*, among many others. He lives in Toronto and welcomes readers at www.michaelrowe.com.

Born in Toronto, KENNETH SHERMAN is the author of three books of prose and ten books of poetry, including the highly acclaimed long poems, *Words for Elephant Man* and *Black River*. His most recent publications are *Wait Time: A Memoir of Cancer*, and the poetry collection, *Jogging with the Great Ray Charles*.

ANTANAS SILEIKA is the author of four books of fiction and a forthcoming memoir. He has been shortlisted for the Leacock Medal for Humour and the Toronto Book Award and two of his novels made *The Globe and Mail*'s lists of the best books of the year. A film adaptation of his novel, *Underground*, is currently under development in Europe. He is the director of The Humber School for Writers.

FRED STENSON is a features editor and columnist at *Alberta Views*. A novelist, non-fiction writer, and film writer, he is the author of over 20 books, including the novel *Who By Fire* (Doubleday Canada, 2014), and a long-time Albertan.

LEONA THEIS lives in Saskatoon. She is the author of *Sightlines*, a collection of linked stories, and *The Art of Salvage*, a novel about messing up and finding hope. Her essays have appeared in *enRoute*, *Brick*, *The New Quarterly* and *Numero Cinq*. Recent fiction includes the prize-winning story "How Sylvie Failed to Become a Better Person through Yoga" in *American Short Fiction*. This printing of "Six Ways" is dedicated to Frank, in memoriam.

ELANA WOLFF is a Toronto-based poet, editor, essayist, translator, and designer and facilitator of therapeutic social art courses. Her poems have appeared in journals and anthologies in Canada, the US, the UK, and France, and have garnered awards. Her essay, "Paging Kafka's Elegist," won *The New Quarterly* 2015 Edna Staebler Personal Essay Contest. Her fifth collection of poems, *Everything Reminds You of Something Else*, is forthcoming with Guernica Editions in spring 2017.

Permission Acknowledgements

Grateful acknowledgment is made to the following for permission to reprint previously published material:

"Dinner with the Vittrekwas" appeared in *PRISM* 54.1 © copyright 2015 by Carleigh Baker. Used with permission of author.

"The Unbelievers" appeared in *Maisonneuve* 58 © copyright 2015 by Graeme Bayliss. Used with permission of author.

"The Skin I'm In" appeared in *Toronto Life* (May 2015) © copyright 2015 by Desmond Cole. Used with permission of author.

"Falling; Fallen" appeared in *Humber Literary Review* 1:2 © copyright 2015 by Krista Foss. Used with permission of author.

"The Fate of Two Brothers" appeared in *Legion Magazine* (January 2015) © copyright 2015 by Don Gillmor. Used with permission of author.

"War and Peace in the Robotic Age" appeared in *Queen's Quarterly* 122:4 © copyright 2015 by Wayne A. Hunt. Used with permission of author.

"A Dozen Cups of the Dead" appeared in *The New Quarterly* 134 © copyright 2015 by Michelle Kaeser. Used with permission of author.

Editors' Biographies

JOSEPH KERTES' first novel, *Winter Tulips*, won the Stephen Leacock Award for Humour. His third novel, *Gratitude*, won a Canadian Jewish Book Award and the US National Jewish Book Award for Fiction. His most recent novel is *The Afterlife of Stars*. Kertes founded Humber College's distinguished creative writing and comedy programs.

CHRISTOPHER DODA is a poet, editor and critic living in Toronto. He is the author of two books of poetry, *Among Ruins* and *Aesthetics Lesson*. His award-winning non-fiction has appeared in journals across Canada and he was on the editorial board of Exile Editions for over ten years.